"What does it mean to be modern?

To be modern is not a fashion, it is

a state. It is necessary to understand

history, and he who understands

history knows how to find continuity

between that which was, that which

is, and that which will be."

Le Corbusier

MOROCCO

MODERN

HERBERT
YPMA

STEWART, TABORI & CHANG
NEW YORK

PAGES 2–3

Zillij, the art of Moroccan ceramics, is a tradition that has survived well over a thousand years of turbulent and eventful history. In the hands of contemporary architects such as Marrakesh-based Charles Boccara, this vivid and exciting art form has been simplified and streamlined into an expression that is now thoroughly at home in a contemporary context. This floor of the terrace of a recently completed villa is a convincing example: graphic and simply composed, it still maintains the colour and geometry that make it uniquely Moroccan.

PAGES 4–5

Designer and architect Bill Willis, an American expatriate who works in Marrakesh, brings to his work the lush, exotic, Oriental beauty of Moroccan culture, tempered and pared down with a Western restraint.

In this detail of his design for a small conversation corner of a Moroccan restaurant at the Tichka Hotel, the choice of a golden monochrome palette highlights and reinforces the typical Moroccan details, such as the striped plastering effect.

PAGES 6–7

Perhaps the most distinctive aspect of Moroccan culture as opposed to other Islamic nations is the extraordinary and ubiquitous use of colour. As Mohammed's followers swept swiftly westwards in the 8th century, they brought with them a culture based on geometric expression (figurative representation is forbidden). The Berbers, inhabitants of the Atlas Mountains which separate Morocco from the rest of Mediterranean North Africa, were quick to become Muslims, but the influence was not all one way. Islamic culture – partic-

ularly architecture and handcraft – acquired a new sense of colour. The Berbers added pink, purple, orange, red and yellow to the existing blue, white and green palette of Islamic culture.

PAGE 8

In a complex outside Marrakesh, situated in a magnificent palm grove that extends for miles, architect Charles Bocarra has created what is, perhaps, Morocco's first 'condo'. Borrowing in style from the classical architecture of ancient Egypt and the distinctive shape of Berber **ksour**, a group of refined town houses, constructed in concrete but plastered in traditional 'mud' render, successfully combine the comforts of modern life – swimming pools, lots of bathrooms, light, space and an indoor/outdoor lifestyle – with the mood, texture and 'ambience' of Morocco's spellbinding history and culture.

To my parents, Carla and Peter, who have given me a more interesting and adventurous life than anyone could possibly hope for.

© 1996 Herbert Ypma

First published in Great Britain in 1996 by Thames and Hudson Ltd, London

Published in 1996 and distributed in the U.S. by
Stewart, Tabori & Chang,
a division of U.S. Media Holdings, Inc.
575 Broadway, New York, NY 10012

Distributed in Canada by General Publishing Co. Ltd.,
30 Lesmill Road, Don Mills, Ontario, Canada M3B 2T6

Library of Congress Catalog Card Number: 96-68726
ISBN: 1-55670-501-8

Printed in Singapore
10 9 8 7 6 5 4 3 2 1

CONTENTS

INTRODUCTION

Morocco is one of the few places on earth where you can have one foot in the biblical past and the other in the 20th century. That is what makes it so special.

It is a country of donkeys and mules and motorbikes and Renaults, where the cry of the *muezzin* calling the faithful to prayer still wafts across the labyrinth-like *medina* of the old city, while the sophisticated young population make calls on their cellular phones from café terraces in the *ville nouvelle*. Traditional *djellabas* and *haiks*, in impossibly bright shades of blue, purple, pink and yellow, mingle with smart suits, couture fashion and jeans. Colourfully ethnic and stylishly urban, Morocco is, above all, a visually sophisticated nation. Its landscape and culture have a distinctive beauty which has impressed artists and travellers alike over the ages. It is a nation that is the result of an impressive historical legacy.

Moroccan culture reached its zenith in the 11th, 12th and 13th centuries when the Almoravid and Almohad dynasties ruled North Africa from Marrakesh to Tunis and most of the southern parts of Spain known as *El Andalus*. The Moors excelled in mathematics, literature and medicine, in pottery, ceramics and woodwork, and they built mosques, minarets and palaces that were the envy of the entire Islamic world.

The achievements of this great cultural flowering, curiously, were preserved by defeat at the hands of the Crusaders in 1492. For almost 500 years Morocco remained closed to outsiders. By the time this unique Islamic nation emerged into the modern world, history had begun to recognize the importance of ancient artistic traditions. Thus the skill of Moroccan craftsmen, already legendary more than a thousand years before, was given fresh relevance. In essence, the crafts have stayed the same, whereas the application has been updated. The skills traditionally used to build and adorn mosques and palaces are now also being employed by contemporary architects and designers for public buildings, houses, restaurants and hotels.

These people, still able to make beautiful things with their hands, are the source of a fascinating style, a synthesis of the traditions of a glorious past and the modern attitudes of a young nation. Unexpected, captivating, colourful, exotic, rich in detail and yet thoroughly contemporary, the work being carried out in Morocco now is as fascinating for us today as it probably was to the uninitiated a thousand years ago. Contemplate the possibilities in our cities if we could still call on all the crafts that existed a millennium ago. Such a scenario is reality in modern Morocco.

1

INTERIORS

We are a curious race. We value our privacy, yet given half a chance we are more than prepared to take a good look around our neighbour's house. How people live creates in us an almost intuitive and insatiable curiosity.

THE

VILLA

MAROC

Essaouira, or Mogador as it was once called, is one of the most famous little places in Morocco. Orson Welles came here when he needed a location for *Othello*, and centuries earlier the Portuguese captured the town in an attempt to dominate Atlantic trade.

It is not hard to see why Welles chose this old fishing port, idyllically situated on a promontory overlooking the Atlantic Ocean. Even today, Essaouira, whether viewed from the sea, from the fort guarding the harbour entrance or from inside the narrow laneways of the old city, is unchanged since the time when it was a Portuguese stronghold.

Filming on *Othello* was continually interrupted by money difficulties, which forced the crew to spend an unexpectedly long sojourn in this old trading post. This was no doubt a source of great glee for the villagers as they filled their coffers with revenue from their long-term guests. To commemorate the film that Welles made (and the money he spent), the town dedicated a square to him, complete with bust.

Long before Welles came here to make a film, the Romans came to make purple. On a tiny island just off the entrance to the harbour, Emperor Juba II established dye works for the production of purple, the most sought-after colour in the Roman Empire. As a symbol of rank and honour, the prestige attached to a purple cloak was unimaginable. Thus the dye works entrusted with this rare and precious commodity were kept strictly low-profile. The tribal inhabitants of Mauritania, as it was then known, were already skilled in preparing dyes from local vegetable and mineral sources. Indigo was used for blues and greens, madder root for red, pomegranate skins for black, saffron and almond leaves for yellow, and tea and henna for red-brown earth tones. This tiny island just off the coast of Essaouira, one of the Iles Purpuraires, was selected because the dye for purple comes from the murex shell.

Such tales typify Morocco's exotic and unexpected historical past. And it is surely one of its most fascinating aspects. History is, literally, all around you. This is probably also one of the reasons why Essaouira's Villa Maroc is such a popular place to stay.

Situated in a mansion in the old city, near the sea and just along a ridiculously narrow alley bordering the old city wall, the Villa Maroc is to be found at the heart of a world described by James Richardson in his *Travels in Morocco*, published in 1860: 'The houses are regularly built, with streets in direct lines, extremely convenient though somewhat narrow. The residences of the consuls and the European merchants are elegant and spacious. There is a large market place, which on days when the market is not held, furnishes a splendid parade, or corso for exercising cavalry.'

The cavalry no longer exercises in the village square, but the markets still exist and, judging from the myriad potions, powders, ointments, baskets, produce, woodwork, handcraft and 'fresh fish' on offer, little else has changed.

The secret of the Villa Maroc's success may be that it provides what can best be described as a 'comfortable cliché'. All the aspects of what one would expect from Morocco are here: strong, saturated colours; the wrought-iron balconies and chandeliers of Spanish Andalusian influence; Moroccan traditions such as *thé à la menthe* (mint tea); beautiful, vivid examples of handcraft, such as rugs, tiles and woodwork, which show off Morocco's artisan traditions; bright light, strange smells and, of course, modern facilities, such as telephones and bathrooms with hot and cold running water. In short, the romance and character of history without the inconvenience. Also, rather cleverly, the Villa has managed to maintain the feel of a house as opposed to that of a hotel. Each bedroom is different, the decoration attractive but simple. Staff are courteous and discreet but not overly visible, and the cooking is done in a normal-size kitchen and only for the one sitting. The entire experience is more akin to staying at someone's house rather than in a hotel; there are no give-away *faux pas* such as mini-bars, air conditioners or shaver points. For the first-time visitor, the Villa Maroc provides an excellent introduction to the colour, craft and style of Morocco; for, despite the predictability of some of these ingredients, it is nonetheless an inspiring example of traditional craft and colour being used very successfully in a contemporary application.

PREVIOUS PAGES (16)
The ubiquitous blue door. Throughout the Mediterranean, doors and shutters are painted various shades of eye-catching blue in keeping with the traditional practice, believed to date back to ancient Egypt, of using colour to ward off evil spirits. **Djoun** *(the plural of* **djinn***, the word for an evil spirit) are meant to be distracted by the blue and therefore prevented from entering the house.*

OPPOSITE PAGE
A typical bedroom of the Villa Maroc, a mansion converted into a particularly charming small hotel in the old sector of town. It makes use of the simplest ingredients to create an authentic atmosphere. Bold use of colour, simple handcraft items, such as the stools and table, and traditional Moroccan textiles for bedspread and blinds cleverly disguise, and successfully help to compensate for, the tiny size of the rooms.

1	2	3	4
5	6	7	8

1

White walls, a piece of simple pottery, the traditional ceiling-hung decorative glass lantern and a typical tiled floor: a peaceful still life that acts as an effective foil for the blaze of bright colour elsewhere.

2

*A stool upholstered with a piece cut from a handwoven Moroccan rug and antique brass pots and containers accompany the traditional Moroccan custom of **thé à la menthe** (mint tea).*

3

Interior light wells, wrought-iron balconies, liberal use of an 'azul blue' paint and terracotta-paved hallways strongly evoke the former presence of the Portuguese, who for the better part of two centuries controlled this Atlantic seaport.

4

Without great extravagance in terms of furniture, antiques or art, the Villa Maroc has created a seductive, bewitching environment through the clever manipulation and control of two very basic elements: light and colour.

5

*In certain areas the Villa looks distinctly Spanish, which is hardly surprising considering that Morocco had, for centuries, a vital and mutually beneficial cultural exchange with the cities of **El Andalus**, the flourishing and sophisticated Islamic sector of southern Spain.*

6

*A Moroccan villa would be incomplete without some area in which the mesmerizing appeal of **zillij**, the Moroccan tradition of mosaic ceramics, was properly exploited.*

7

Traditional mint tea, an important feature of Moroccan daily life, lanterns, a fireplace, rugs in shades of rich red – these are the ingredients that create a completely different atmosphere at night, in powerful contrast to the bright light and colours of daytime Essaouira.

8

Made from the branches of the oleander, which grows in wild abundance throughout Morocco, these are examples of the ubiquitous Moroccan chair. Either in their natural state or painted Asilah green (as with this chair on the roof terrace of the Villa Maroc), they appear in all houses, whether rich or poor.

OPPOSITE PAGE

*In another bedroom, a more serene side of Moroccan culture is represented. Instead of bold colours, the beds are decorated with the motif found on Berber tents. The Moroccan tile tradition, taken over from the Moors of **El Andalus** when they were forced to flee southern Spain in 1492, is represented by the typical unglazed clay-tile floor.*

DAR
TAMSNA'S
TOBACCO
TADLEKT

Dar Tamsna is a house that captures the true spirit of Morocco. Giorgio Armani, Donna Karan, Gianfranco Ferré and a host of other taste-makers have stayed as guests, and their comments in the celebrity-studded guest book attest to the fact that this house comes as close as any to providing the essential Moroccan experience.

A remarkable feat, given that the house was found by the present owners, less than a decade ago, as 'a concrete block with four walls and no roof' on an abandoned site.

Seduced by the heady atmosphere of Marrakesh, the Loum family discovered two hectares of abandoned property with a half-built house in the very desirable *milieu* of the Marrakesh Palmerai.

Enthralled by the challenge of making something out of a forlorn concrete shell, Meryanne Loum took periodic breaks from her career as a Paris-based lawyer to create a holiday home in Marrakesh. Fascinated by the culture and history of this exotic North African nation, she immersed herself in the traditions of Islamic craft in Moroccan architecture. She became a regular visitor to the *souks* (markets) and, with André Paccard's definitive volumes on the artisan skills of Morocco always to hand, began to commission local craftsmen to produce furniture, finishes and detailing true to the nation's cultural heritage.

With great originality and invention, she adapted authentic Moroccan ingredients for workable contemporary application: *moushrabiyas* (wooden screens), exquisitely carved doors of monumental proportions, *zillij* (cut-tile mosaic), antique lanterns, old tea containers, cedar fretwork, custom-made dark copper pots, tea tables with inlay *zillij* tops, and of course the ubiquitous Moroccan rugs, but this time cut into strips and sewn as borders onto massive lengths of plain canvas curtains. What has ultimately been created is a beautiful example of how the cultural traditions of a nation can be kept alive through reinterpretation.

Perhaps the most interesting example of a Moroccan tradition reinterpreted for modern use in Meryanne Loum's house is *tadlekt*, a polished wall finish that has literally come out of the steam room and into the parlour. Almost as old as the tradition of the *hammam* (steam room) itself is this technique employed to create waterproof,

steamproof walls. The floors of the *hammam* are traditionally laid in sheets of polished marble and a fire is lit underneath to heat the stone. Water is then thrown onto the marble, creating steam. The combination of heat and moisture has always made the wall finish problematic. Both marble cladding and mosaic tiling would be impractical; the traditional solution has been to finish the walls in *tadlekt*, a lime-dust plastering technique that gives a hard, waterproof finish.

The process is lengthy but straightforward. First, walls usually made of mud bricks are trowelled in a plaster of powdered limestone with a small amount of coloured dust mixed in to provide the desired colour. After the plaster has set, it is painstakingly polished with flat river stones approximately the size of a hand. The polishing, a backbreaking chore, makes the plaster as hard as marble. Then, to seal the material further, the surfaces are painted with egg white to glaze them. Finally, the walls are polished with a cake of locally made black soap – the soap is high in oil content and fills up minute fissures which could otherwise let moisture through. It also adds character, highlighting faults in the way that the grain of timber is accentuated by staining.

The tobacco-coloured walls of Dar Tamsna show an appreciation of Moroccan skills and they benefit from being presented in a Western context. This type of translation is essential to a deeper understanding and appreciation of other cultures.

PREVIOUS PAGE (24)
*'Sophisticated, restrained and beautifully detailed' describes not just this bedroom fireplace at Dar Tamsna, but applies equally to the entire estate. Moroccan ingredients are used sparingly. **Zillij** is reduced to a single colour so as not to compete with the wonderful lustre of the walls finished in **tadlekt**. Simple drawings of Arabic life were found in the Paris flea markets.*

PREVIOUS PAGES (26–27)
The main living area of Dar Tamsna is a tranquil, tobacco-coloured retreat away from the bright light and heat of Marrakesh, accented with a collection of beautiful antiques
*and bibelots, predominantly in the Arabic style. Texture and finish play an important role in making the unusual colour palette a success. The walls glow with the hand-polished sheen of **tadlekt** and the floors throughout are of polished marble. The rugs are Turkish **kilims** purchased in Paris, but the pottery and silver and brass containers were found in the Marrakesh **souks**. The larger pots in the corner, the giant candlesticks on the table and most of the furniture were commissioned from local craftsmen.*

OPPOSITE
Light streams through the shutters into a corner of the vast living room, which is often used
*for afternoon tea. The majestic cupboard is originally Syrian and features an elaborate inlay of mother of pearl, which reflects light into the room. Green paisley fabric, a Kashmiri throw, the warm tones of Turkish **kilims** and the **tadlekt** walls create a seductively Oriental atmosphere.*

FOLLOWING PAGES (30–31)
A view of the house and swimming pool from the garden highlights the powerful symmetry, a feature derived from the strictly geometric tendencies of Islamic architecture. Upstairs, the two wings of the house are divided by an outdoor gazebo, square in shape and topped by a decorative timber structure.

1	2	3	4	5	6
7	8	9	10	11	12
13	14	15	16	17	18

PHOTOS IN ORDER OF
APPEARANCE – PREVIOUS PAGES (32–33)

1 & 13

Moroccan ingredients such as Berber pottery are used sparingly to create still lifes throughout the house. The iron pots in photo 13 were custom-made to Meryanne Loum's designs.

2

Zillij *– the Moroccan art of cut-tile mosaic – has been used in a simpler, more contemporary manner. This panel is set like a rug into a brown marble floor.*

3 & 5

The Moroccan sense of colour derives from nature. The garden plays a very important role in Islamic culture. Bougainvilleas turn the villas of Marrakesh into an explosion of colour in April when they blossom.

4

The yellow bathroom highlights Meryanne Loum's great skill in utilizing Moroccan colour and detail in a contemporary, modern manner.

6

Antique tin containers, originally used in the serving of traditional mint tea, were found in the ***souks*** *of Marrakesh.*

7 & 18

Despite her penchant for all things Moroccan, the rugs used throughout Dar Tamsna are Turkish ***kilims***. *The antique brass lamp is from a mosque.*

8

Surrounded by the lush greens of a splendid garden, Dar Tamsna's architecture occasionally peeks through the decorous growth of palm trees and bougainvilleas.

9

Set beneath an arcade of traditional Moroccan Islamic arches are white cotton cushions and simple steel chairs which provide the setting for afternoon tea out of the midday heat.

10 & 14

Old copper containers originally intended for serving tea are used to decorate a mosaic tiled fireplace in one room and a bathroom in another.

11

The first-floor balcony overlooking Dar Tamsna's swimming pool and olive grove is another idyllic setting for tea.

12

Traditional Moroccan brick masonry, ***zillij*** *and Moroccan woodwork are deeply ingrained local cultural signatures that have been utilized by Meryanne Loum in a sophisticated and restrained manner.*

15 & 16

Moushrabiyas, *the traditional Islamic screens originally meant to keep the women of the house from view, are used in Dar Tamsna for decorative effect and add to the authenticity of the ambience.*

17

Attention to detail is a sure sign of successful design and decoration. Even the soap dishes at Dar Tamsna are chosen from traditional Moroccan pottery craft.

OPPOSITE PAGE

Overlooking the entire Palmerai, the palm grove on the outskirts of Marrakesh, the roof of Dar Tamsna is used for special occasions, when it is decorated with layer upon layer of beautiful rugs, large cushions, roses and typical Moroccan lanterns. The effect is straight out of the 'Thousand and One Nights'.

AN
AMERICAN
IN
MARRAKESH

Some of the most extraordinary interiors in the world are in Marrakesh, and perhaps the most exotic and seductive of all of these are the interiors designed by Bill Willis.

An expatriate American, Bill Willis has lived in Marrakesh for the better part of 28 years. Originally from Tennessee, he studied at Columbia University, the famed Ecole des Beaux-Arts in Paris and the Cooper Design Union in New York, before coming on a visit to Marrakesh with Paul Getty.

Completely captivated by Morocco, he decided to stay.

With an eye for detail and a passion for the ingredients of Morroco's architecture, design and artisan history, Willis has forged a style that is all his own; a style that is now widely copied and one that is popular, interestingly, with both his Moroccan clients and his European customers (who build mainly second residences). Through his work for distinguished clients, people like Yves Saint Laurent, Morocco's top industrialists and Paul Getty and the Rothschilds, he has over the years become something of an authority on Moroccan history and tradition and its vast wealth of craft. These are the very ingredients that he chooses to work with and they form the decorative foundations of his work.

Like architect Charles Boccara, with whom he worked on the design of the Tichka Hotel, he prefers to draw most of his historical references from the golden age of Moroccan culture, the Almoravid and Almohad dynasties of the 11th–13th centuries.

In his interiors one finds the distinctive arches, the elaborately painted woodwork, the fanciful and complex geometric patterns of mosaic tiling and the soaring ceilings adorned with extraordinary plaster carving: all astonishing in their complexity, intricacy and beauty, and all originated in Morocco's golden age.

Bill Willis's interiors suit Marrakesh; they are celebrations of their unique location, for, despite the fact that this city has its share of cellular phones, German cars and European fashion, Marrakesh also still has its snake charmers, monkeys, dancers, acrobats, *souks* and the labyrinthine *medina*. Marrakesh is a city like no other. It embodies the spirit of Morocco and Willis is convinced that design needs to recognize and indeed celebrate this fact.

Much in the manner that American author Paul Bowles stimulated interest in Morocco with his novel *The Sheltering Sky*, Bill Willis has used his distinctive visual sense to generate popular interest in Moroccan craft. His interiors have almost single-handedly reintroduced a preference for artisan traditions.

Yet there is nothing nostalgic or melancholy about his enthusiasm for Moroccan culture. The lessons he has learned are all applied in a strictly modern manner. He is certainly not recreating historical interiors; in fact, in his opinion the *kasbahs* and *riyadhs* of old are far too much. Layer upon layer of intricate mosaics, woodwork and plaster carving were piled on one another like rugs in a bazaar. Even very grand spaces were, as a result, often buried in a carnival of decorative effects. In traditional terms, more was never enough! Even today, Willis will confide, many Moroccans just don't know when to stop.

Thus, in addition to rekindling an age-old love affair with decorative craft, this American in Marrakesh is credited with having introduced a new ingredient to the equation, namely: restraint.

PREVIOUS PAGE (36)
Deep within the **medina**, *the ancient, maze-like inner city of Marrakesh, Bill Willis created an exquisite mansion for an Argentinian aristocrat and filled it with lots of decorative delights. This fireplace on the first floor, shaped like an onion-domed minaret, combines the beauty of* **zillij** *(mosaic tiling) and the textural lustre of* **tadlekt** *(polished, tinted lime render) in two colour stripes.*

PREVIOUS PAGES (38–39)
Johara, the Tichka Hotel's restaurant, provided Willis with an opportunity to try many of his signature design touches in the commercial arena. His special brand of decorative magic leaves all newcomers to the restaurant awestruck. Blue **tadlekt** *(polished and unpolished in alternating stripes),* **zillij** *floors, a marble fireplace in the shape of an arch, cobalt-blue silk upholstery and ornate wall decoration conspire to create an exotic effect.*

OPPOSITE
Thé à la menthe *(mint tea) is a strong cultural tradition in Morocco. This setting highlights some of the key elements of Moroccan style that Bill Willis has managed to incorporate successfully into his work. Tables are inlaid with* **zillij**. *The Berber sense of colour is reflected in the striped textile, and the silver metalwork tradition in the handworked teapot and typical raised tray.*

FOLLOWING PAGE (42)
Viewed directly from below, the most impressive aspect of the Tichka Hotel, in design and architecture, is definitely the massive, octagonal reception lobby. Topped with an ornate, intricately painted dome in the tradition of the great painted ceilings of historical Moroccan architecture, this space represents almost the perfect combination of a tremendous and cleverly conceived volume, a grand area that all the floors leading to all the rooms look down into, the signature of a talented architect (Charles Boccara) and the decorative detailing that is the signature of designer Bill Willis.

FOLLOWING PAGES (44–45)
Steps to the roof of a **medina** *villa are typical of designer Bill Willis's attention to detail. Resident now in Marrakesh for the better part of 28 years, he is a faithful student of Moroccan history and his work is filled with references to the golden age of Moroccan culture. Despite his command and understanding of all the Moroccan craft disciplines, Willis still studiously avoids the point where it all becomes too much.*

"The Alhambra...

is an eternal proof of how art

can transfigure the poverty of materials

by the subtlety of its invention."

Emilio Garciá Gómez

The World of Islam, edited by Bernard Lewis, 1976

MUD

MODERN

The contemporary architecture scene in Marrakesh is quite lively, particularly in the Palmerai, an extensive area that is home to one of the most impressive palm groves in North Africa. For Morocco's new wave of architects this Palmerai has become, in the last ten years, a laboratory for the development of an appropriate contemporary Moroccan architectural style. Two of the main protagonists are Charles Boccara, whose work is discussed in detail in the final chapter of this book, and his one-time protégé, now working independently, Elie Mouyal.

Blessed with rich fertile clay and sitting on top of a substantial network of artesian wells, the Palmerai is one of the finest sections of real estate in North Africa – an observation first made by Luis de Marmol in 1573 in his published account of Marrakesh: 'It is a great city, the best situated in all Africa, in a fine plain, five or six leagues from the Atlas Mountains, surrounded by the richest countryside of all Mauritania. It is clear that this city is the work of great masters because the design is as good as its execution.'

The Palmerai is also a model of fine town planning. Only in the last 20 years or so has King Hassan II allowed this natural wonder to be developed, and then strictly along ecologically sound guidelines. Land is only available in parcels of more than one hectare and any building that takes place is not allowed to interfere with, damage or destroy existing palm trees. This has effectively prevented the activities of greedy property developers and ensured that the houses, all a considerable distance away from their neighbours, do not impair the natural beauty of this palm grove. Space, responsible town planning, an idyllic natural setting, close proximity to the heart of one of Morocco's most exciting cities, a plentiful source of clean water and a red clay soil that when irrigated will grow almost anything – these factors combine to make this one of the most exciting places to build.

Despite its extraordinary history and impressive cultural heritage, Morocco is in many ways a new nation. Having emerged from centuries of self-imposed exile, it knows only the extremes of the very old and the really new. Unlike most other modern nations, compromise and mediocrity have not had a chance to creep in.

Therefore the challenge for architects like Elie Mouyal is to combine the Hispano-Mauresque legacy with the tradition of mud architecture for contemporary purposes.

Continuing in the direction in which his studies took him, Mouyal is working on a means of making 'earth' construction a viable alternative for building in southern Morocco. The success of this search, he would be the first to admit, is largely conditional upon finding a client willing to participate in the same experiment. He found just such a benefactor in Prince Panatovski. A member of the deposed royal family of Poland and a long-time resident of Paris, Panatovski commissioned Mouyal to design and build a second home for him in a prime location within the Palmerai. The result is a house that is undeniably modern yet unmistakably Moroccan.

Perhaps unexpectedly, especially for colour-saturated Morocco, this house is entirely monochrome: interior and exterior − all walls, floors and ceilings − are a warm, earthy brown. It is a house where textures and shapes play the predominant decorative and constructional role. This recalls the traditional Berber mud dwellings. *Kasbahs* and *ksour* in southern Morocco are the colour of the local clay, inside and out. Only weavings and the odd painted door and window are used to add colour.

Mouyal's experiments with Marrakesh clay established that it had all the necessary ingredients to make adobe bricks for vaulting and pisé bricks for walls; thus, handmade bricks from local clay were used throughout.

Four centuries earlier, Luis de Marmol had drawn the same conclusion in his *Descripcion general de Affrica*: 'The city of Marrakesh is enclosed in fine walls, made of lime and sand, mixed with earth which makes them so hard that if they are struck by a pick, they give forth a spark as does a flint.'

PREVIOUS PAGE (46)
Set against the darkened sky of a thunderstorm at sunset, the modern villa designed for Prince Panatovski by Marrakesh-based architect Elie Mouyal has set Arabic shapes and symbols within a pared-down cubic structure.

PREVIOUS PAGES (48–49)
The most astonishing feature of the main living area is the extraordinarily beautiful vaulting of the ceiling. The entire space has avoided colour to allow the eye to focus on shapes and textures. There is a hard floor comprising an intricate pattern of monochrome clay-coloured tiles. The substantial pillars are finished in **tadlekt**.

OPPOSITE
The ingredients of the interior have been kept simple and authentic. The lamps are Moroccan and were purchased from the **souks**, *as were the pottery and ceramics adorning the shelves on either side of the fireplace. The painting is by famous expat French artist Jacques Majorelle. A sense of space and the enveloping warmth of earthy finishes create the mood of this house.*

FOLLOWING PAGE (52)
The veranda adjoining the living area is used for warm-weather entertaining. Floors are of **tadlekt**, *with a pattern of inlaid masonry tiles. In the heat of the day the outdoor curtains keep out direct sunlight and with the desert chill setting in for the evening there is an outdoor fireplace, constructed in an authentically Moroccan brick pattern.*

"Fez is Europe but closed;

Marrakesh is Africa but open.

Fez is black, white and grey;

Marrakesh is red."

John Gunther, *Inside Africa*, 1955

THE
CAID'S
PLEASURE PAVILION

On the road to Asmizmiz, only a half-hour's journey from Marrakesh, lies Dar El Caid, an Islamic pleasure garden situated between the ruins of one *kasbah* and the mud towers of another, in a village that carries one back to another millennium, where the donkey is transport and the mule is the truck.

It was this Morocco that captured the imagination of Gilles Berthomme. An inveterate globe-trotter and a bit of a 'hippy', Gilles has seen more countries than most people could hope to read about in *National Geographic*. Having sold his business in Biarritz, he came to Morocco with plans to retire in the Marrakesh *medina*. Bewitched by the sights, sounds and smells of its dark, labyrinthine passages, he set out to do the impossible: to get to know his way around the *medina*. There are Moroccans who have lived in Marrakesh all their lives who do not know their way around it. Determined, wily and resourceful, Gilles arrived with his mountain bike and each day for six months pedalled his way across and around the *medina*. He remained on the lookout for a suitable *riyadh* (literally, a 'square', as these houses are built around a square courtyard) but eventually heard about a derelict pleasure pavilion in a small village hugging the base of the Atlas not far from Marrakesh.

Its history is fascinating: situated in the heart of Berber tribal territory, the village had been the property of a Caid who was continually warring with a rival. The rival triumphed and, in the long-standing tradition of the Berber clans, the winner took all and the loser, literally, lost all. The defeated Caid's *kasbah* was destroyed, his harem dispersed, his children enslaved, and once he had lived to see all this misery, he was beheaded. The new Caid then proceeded to build a *kasbah* for himself directly opposite the ruins of the one he had destroyed. He prospered and added a pleasure garden, situated exactly between the two *kasbahs*. Whenever he looked up from his beautifully manicured hectare of garden (with its four adjoining pavilions, each to house, presumably, a different concubine), he would see the majesty of the snow-capped peaks of the Atlas Mountains, the ruins of his old rival's *kasbah* and the magnificence of his new one – fitting reminders of the spoils of his glorious victory.

It was this same pleasure garden that Gilles found in a neglected state when curiosity prompted his first visit two years ago. Enchanted by the setting and excited

by the potential of such an extraordinary place, he decided then and there that he would devote all his energy to restoring its former beauty and elegance. The *medina* and retirement were forgotten as he set about negotiating a long-term lease with the Caid's descendants, who had themselves fallen on hard times. This done, he started the monumental task of renovating a structure the size of an entire city block.

Two years later Gilles is close to knowing how the first Caid felt. The task has almost broken him. The physical, mental and financial strain has been relentless and the enormity of the task has just about drained his resources. But the result will make it all worthwhile. Architecturally, the building work has painstakingly reproduced traditional methods, detailing and features. And the garden, which has been entirely replanted, is starting to show glimpses of its former verdant glory. In the process Gilles has also become very fit. The enclosed area contains four separate buildings; the distance between each is considerable. The walk from his bedroom 'building' to the one housing the kitchen is roughly the length of a football field.

With a view to receiving paying guests, Gilles has made sure that the facilities, in contrast to the architecture, are anything but ancient. Each of the three gargantuan suites has its own bathroom, complete with hot and cold running water and Western-style toilets. The walls are finished in lustrous *tadlekt* and the 6- or 7-metre-high (20–23 feet) ceilings feature the distinctive reed and timber thatch of tradition.

There is a swimming pool set into the corner of the garden, and two raised gazebos have been designed to provide a platform from which to view the surrounding biblical countryside while taking breakfast. But the overriding appeal of Dar El Caid must surely be the experience of it all: here, you can wake up, have a shower, eat some breakfast, open the gate and step two thousand years back in time.

PREVIOUS PAGE (54)
Situated in the foothills of the Atlas Mountains, the magnificent Islamic pleasure garden of Dar El Caid is watched over by the crumbling remains of the Caid's original **kasbah**.

PREVIOUS PAGES (56–57)
A domed pavilion in the centre of the pleasure garden was constructed from the remains of sets left behind after the filming of Martin Scorsese's 'The Last Temptation of Christ'. The

raised, canopied structure set against the wall was constructed as the ideal spot from which to enjoy a view of the snow-capped Atlas while taking breakfast.

OPPOSITE
The interiors of Dar El Caid are furnished simply and appropriately; the furniture was crafted in the **souks** *of Marrakesh, and the bathrooms, of which a glimpse can be seen through the arch, consist entirely of* **tadlekt**,

the traditional waterproof finish of the **hammam**. *The rooms are all of magnificent proportions with towering ceilings.*

FOLLOWING PAGES (60–61)
In true Islamic fashion, the pleasure garden of Dar El Caid has hedge-lined, raised pathways leading to each of its four identical pavilions. These are all distinguished by an entrance of three soaring arches and they form the axis points of this geometrically configured enclosure.

2

ORIGINS

None of us exists in a vacuum. Everything about us, where we live and how we live, is inextricably linked to how our forebears lived. Connected to our ancestors via distinct forms, patterns, rhythms and shapes, we belong to societies that are in a continuing balancing act between forging forward and looking back. We cannot escape history and tradition.

KSOUR

KASBAHS

THE MUD ARCHITECTURE OF THE BERBERS

A Land of Mud Castles, the title of Jim Ingram's 1952 book, is an apt and particularly vivid description of the region of Morocco dominated by the Berber clans.

The mud brick architecture of the forts and palaces scattered along the oases of the Sahara desert and through the valleys of the formidable Atlas Mountains is an awe-inspiring reminder of the 'feudal' way of life that predominated in this area right up until the 1950s. The materials and forms of these architectural wonders in mud reappear time and time again in Morocco's modern design.

The Berbers were the original inhabitants of Morocco, long before the Romans established their outpost of Volubilis in 'Mauritania'. Fiercely independent, they submit only to their own strict councils called *Jemmaa* and, even today, few Berbers speak Arabic. Their dislike of external authority has meant that Morocco has always had to be ruled as two separate entities. From the earliest times, Morocco was divided into the *Bled El Makhzen* and the *Bled Es Siba*. The *Makhzen* included the imperial cities, coastal ports and the plains in between. The rest, the *Bled Es Siba*, has always been the ungovernable portion: the domain of the Berbers.

Berbers have always dominated the Atlas and the southern Sahara, which has allowed them to control the trade route of the famous *caravanserai*. Right up until the establishment of the French protectorate earlier this century, they were able to exact a significant toll for safe passage along the desert oases and over the few navigable Atlas mountain passes that connect sub-Saharan Africa with Marrakesh. The Berbers' fortified 'mud castles' were situated strategically along the oases to provide a safe haven for travelling merchants, but at a price. The traders had little choice – there were only very few roads to Marrakesh and the Berbers controlled all of them. No merchant with any sense would risk his valuable merchandise by sleeping out in the open.

The typical fortified village built by the Berbers from 'mud' bricks, reinforced with lime, is called a *ksar*, or *ksour* in the plural. A *kasbah* is virtually the same as a *ksar* except that it is usually the domain of a single family (a private castle) as opposed to a whole village. These heavily fortified fortresses were built as much to protect the

Berbers against one another as to protect the *caravanserai* from marauding bandits. History books abound with tales of the constant warring between rival factions. In his book *Morocco That Was*, Walter Harris describes an incident in which the Glaoua, one of the fiercest Berber clans, laid siege to a rival's *kasbah*, hunted down the leader, cut off his head and then rode round and round the *kasbah* walls with the newly severed head on the tip of a lance for all to see. 'If you open the gates,' the Glaoua promised, 'this fate will not await you.' Yet, having been let in, the Glaoua proceeded to decapitate everyone within, on the grounds that they had waited too long before answering.

These ancient structures that predominate in southern Morocco are a vivid testament to the power of the Berbers. Interestingly, because of the materials used to build these structures – pisé or mud – it is impossible to tell if a particular building is ten or a hundred years old. Walter Harris comments that a popular way to break down the defences of a 'mud castle' was to re-route a river and wait for the castle's foundations to collapse. Thus, these structures have had to be replaced often, and each time the same materials, forms and decorations have been used, leading to an architectural signature so consistent and simultaneously so distinctive that it comes as no surprise that it is incorporated into the expression of a modern Morrocan architectural style.

"It had little of the elaborate grace of the earlier Glaoua kasbahs at Telouet,

in which the architectural influence of the Dra and Dadès valleys

– probably relics of the Phoenician colonists –

predominated in tapering towers and intricate decoration."

Gavin Maxwell, *Lords of the Atlas*
referring to the Glaoua stronghold at Telouet

PREVIOUS PAGE (64)

*Long before the Romans came to the **Maghreb**, the Arab term for the countries of North Africa, the Berbers had settled here. Berbers played a key role in the development of trade with sub-Saharan Africa. Caravans loaded with precious gold, amber, ostrich feathers, animal skins and slaves would head to the great southern trading city of Marrakesh, and these 'mud forts' would provide – at a price – a safe haven for the valuable camel trains.*

PREVIOUS PAGES (66–67)

*Unlike the discreet Arab architecture which gives nothing away from the outside, **kasbahs** (single-family fortresses) and **ksour** (fortified villages) are often embellished with bold, geometric motifs. Berbers believe not only in the meditative and aesthetic aspect of decoration but also in its supernatural power. Decoration is believed to hold a talismanic power known as **baraka**, a means of deflecting the dreaded evil eye.*

OPPOSITE

*Built of mud, some of Morocco's most attractive **ksour** (plural of **ksar**) cling to the sides of the Dadès valley in the southern Sahara, surrounded by hundreds of acres of date palms and fruit trees. Because of the continual renewal necessary with the use of such a building material, it is impossible to determine how old these structures really are, but it is safe to say that they have changed little over the past two thousand years.*

THE ISLAMIC INFLUENCE IN THE
MAGHREB
EL
AQSA

When General Oqba Ibn Nafi rode fully armed into the Atlantic in AD 680 to proclaim, with sword raised to Allah, that 'he could go no further', it marked the dramatic arrival of Islam in Morocco. Henceforth, this newly conquered Islamic frontier would be known as the *Maghreb El Aqsa* – 'the land furthest west'.

The people of the Middle East and North Africa embraced Islam almost immediately. The appeal of this new religion was its directness. Believers had only to follow the five pillars of faith: prayer five times a day; the observance of *Ramadan*, a month of fasting during daylight hours; pilgrimage to Mecca, which must be undertaken at least once in a lifetime; the giving of alms to the poor and needy; and *Shahada*, the acceptance that 'there is no god but God and Mohammed is his prophet'. Islam would prove to have the single greatest influence in Morocco's long and complex history.

Previously, Morocco had resisted any efforts to establish centralized government; even the Romans stopped trying to impose order on the stubborn tribes that inhabited this land (which gave rise to their being called *barbari*, whence 'Berbers'). Only Islam was successful in uniting Morocco's inhabitants.

The first dynasty to bring together the feuding principalities of both the Arabs and the Berbers was the Idrissids. Moulay Idriss, the great-grandson of the prophet Mohammed, established the infrastructure of this Arab kingdom which is still the basis of government in Morocco today. He was also the first leader to be recognized as the *Imam*, the spiritual as well as the political leader of the people.

The reign of Moulay Idriss II is seen as the beginning of Morocco's golden age. He established the city of Fez as the seat of government and endowed it with a breathtaking legacy of buildings, including, most importantly, Quaraouyine University. The latter was renowned at the time as one of the three greatest universities in the world. It pioneered studies in mathematics and other sciences, and its structure, particularly its division into residential colleges, was adopted by Salamanca, Bologna and later Oxford.

But this cultural flowering was followed by chaos, fragmentation and decadence, which continued until the emergence of a new dynasty, when for the first time in Morocco's turbulent history the Berbers took control. From the nomadic regions of the south came the founders of one of the most powerful and influential dynasties of the Islamic world. The successive Berber dynasties of the Almoravids and the Almohads, although lasting only just over 200 years, represent a period when Morocco was pre-eminent in all Islam, forging an empire that stretched east to present-day Libya, south to Senegal and north as far as the Pyrenees. The Almoravids were led by a reforming zealot, Youssef Bin Tachfine, who, preaching a return to the orthodoxy of Islam, launched an almighty *Jihad* (holy war) and established his seat, unlike earlier leaders, at Marrakesh.

From here the fierce Moors established control over most of North Africa before they crossed over into Spain at the invitation of Andalusia's Muslims, who had just lost the battle for Toledo to the Christians. The Almoravids placed governors in the cities of Seville and Granada and the Almohads actually moved their capital from Marrakesh to Seville.

The strong, pious leadership of the Berber dynasties and the sophisticated art, architecture and craft of the Andalusian Muslims proved a powerful combination. The most magnificent examples of Islamic architecture were built during their rule, including the magnificent gateways and minarets of Seville and the Koutoubia mosque in Marrakesh.

However, imperial expansion once again precipitated disintegration. Under constant pressure from crusading Christians, the Moorish presence in Spain was reduced to just Granada while the provinces in Morocco were once again returning to the rule of local tribes. In this period of instability, yet another tribesman, Abd al-Haqq, rose to power and established the Merinid dynasty. Although the Merinids ruled for well over 300 years, Moroccan political influence continued to decline. *El Andalus* had almost all been lost to the Christians and, in spite of efforts to re-establish a power-

PREVIOUS PAGE (70)
Rising majestically from the centre of Marrakesh, the Koutoubia minaret was constructed by Sultan Yacoub El Mansour (1184–1199) of the Almohad dynasty. Nearly 70 metres high, its proportions have had a widespread influence on Moroccan architecture. The three gilt

balls at the summit, originally thought to have been gold (they are copper), are believed to be a gift from the Sultan's wife as penance for breaking her **Ramadan** *fast.*

OPPOSITE
Historically, the most magnificent examples of the skills of

Moroccan craftsmen were reserved for the mosques and **medersas** *(colleges or seminaries) of Islam. In the El Atterin* **medersa** *of Quaraouyine University in Fez, the walls are decorated with a pattern in* **zillij** *known as* **darj w ktaf**, *with a border of calligraphy. The pattern is still being used today.*

base, the Merinids were reduced to protecting their only remaining kingdom of Granada. They did, however, contribute handsomely in the way of buildings: for instance, the impressive *medersas* or colleges of Quaraouyine University in Fez, which can still be viewed in their original splendour.

By the time of the Wattasid dynasty, the *Maghreb* had shrunk to a shadow of its former self. Algeria and Tunisia had long been lost to the growing might of the Ottoman Empire, Granada fell to Ferdinand and Isabella in 1492, and Portugal, a powerful trading nation, had laid claim to its coastal seaports. Faced with the shock of defeat, Morocco turned to isolation. It became an introverted nation, suspicious of foreigners, summed up in the Moroccan proverb, 'A man bitten by a snake is afraid of the coiled rope'.

Yet, once again, a new power emerged amidst the turmoil. Although commanding a much-reduced empire, the Saadian dynasty is noteworthy if only for marking the end of Berber rule. It was the first Arabic dynasty since the Idrissids.

Morocco's last stab at imperial glory came with the Alaouite dynasty under the notorious Moulay Ismail. His cruelty was legendary: he killed often and indiscriminately. It was not unusual for him to slice off the heads of his own guards simply to test the sharpness of his blade. Unfortunately, Ismail's thirst for 'blood sport' overshadowed the fact that he was also a great builder. The wealth he accumulated from instigating a programme of taxation resulted in a string of *kasbahs*, and in Meknès, his imperial capital, he built a palace of a size and grandeur to match Versailles.

Moulay Ismail's reputation was such that it may have temporarily dissuaded European powers from carving up the *Maghreb El Aqsa* for their own colonial ends. Nevertheless, by the end of the Napoleonic Wars in Europe, Britain, France, Spain and Germany were all looking to establish themselves in Africa.

Because of its isolation, Morocco had lost touch with the times, and a lame attempt to help the Ottomans, fellow Muslims in Algeria, only demonstrated how powerless they were against the technologically superior Europeans. Moroccan warfare was still waged in medieval fashion, on horseback, with single-shot rifles that had to be reloaded with a powder horn. With their beautifully inlaid rifle butts and superb horses and riding skills, it was an elegant and supremely stylish way to do battle but completely ineffective against the repeating rifles and revolvers of the 'Christian Dogs'.

OPPOSITE

*The woodwork in the mosques and **medersas** of Morocco's old imperial cities attest to the exquisite workmanship of the Moroccan artisan. Utilizing a vocabulary that includes calligraphy, as well as polygonal, arabesque, floral and other motifs of Islamic art, this elaborate woodwork, set against predominantly white stucco walls, creates a powerful visual effect.*

By the time Morocco had become a French protectorate in 1912, the reigning Sultan, Moulay Hafid, another Alaouite, was nothing more than a puppet for the French military regime. However, Morocco was fortunate to have General Lyautey as its first Governor General. With his policy of 'Do not offend a single tradition, do not change a single habit', the achievements of more than a thousand years were, thankfully, preserved. The old imperial cities were left largely intact, with the *villes nouvelles* built around their old walls mainly to house the influx of European settlers and administrators. The French also set about building roads and railways and introducing other technological necessities, such as electrical power and irrigation.

Ironically, it was the French insistence on providing a system of education that virtually guaranteed Moroccan independence. Western-trained Moroccans were the first to call for self-rule, and despite their initial resistance to *Istiqlal* (the independence movement), the French eventually relented in 1956. Mohammed V, a descendant of Moulay Ismail, took the throne and, in a move more in line with a modern nation, changed his title to King, the title that passed to his son, Hassan II, in 1961.

Throughout this eventful period, the path of Morocco's architecture and arts remained relatively straight. It managed to define an architectural style that was to become the envy of the Arab world. Even in the most turbulent of times, the artisans and craftsmen of Morocco had continued to develop their skills in mosaic tiling, wood and stucco carving, carpentry and stone masonry.

The present monarch, King Hassan II, is acutely aware of the power and value of these traditional skills and he has, from the very beginning of his reign, instituted many programmes and incentives to revive and update these traditions – ingredients of a fascinating culture.

"God is beautiful and loves Beauty!"

Hadith (saying) of the prophet Mohammed

OPPOSITE
Morocco's most splendid decorative artifacts were at one time limited to just two patrons: the mosque and the royal family. This beautifully ornate lantern, one of a pair that adorns the walls of a contemporary villa in Marrakesh, was originally created for use in a mosque. The three decorative balls on top are a miniature reference to the gold balls that sit atop Marrakesh's most famous minaret, the Koutoubia.

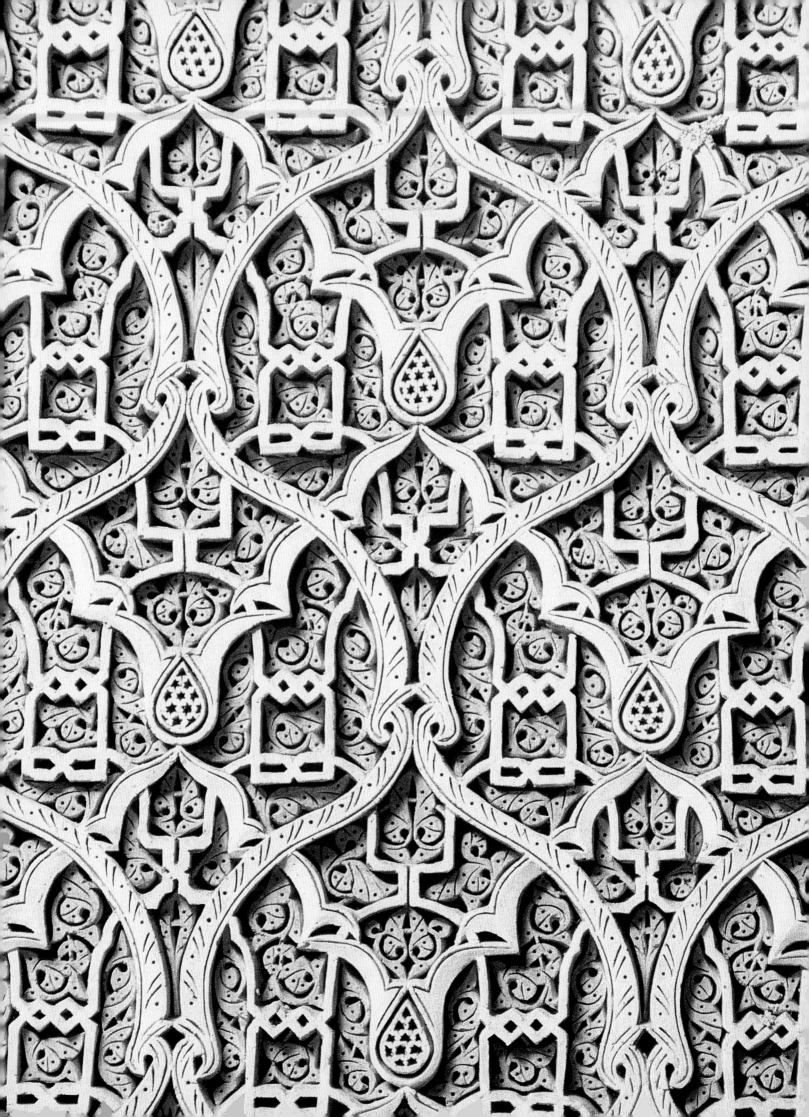

3

COLOURS

Colour plays a distinct role in shaping the visual culture of a city or country. It is one of the oldest forms of communication known, and we are attracted to it like magpies to a shiny object. Colour is simple and pure.

A
PEACOCK
IN THE
WILD

To be around after the rain in Morocco is to understand its love affair with colour.

The dusty, parched earth, cracked like glazed pottery, turns a deep red and, within 24 hours, previously barren plains sport a stubble of green growth. Three days later the whole landscape is awash with carpets of bright colour. Entire fields of brilliant saffron, vivid orange, ox-blood red, egg-yolk yellow, vermilion, pink, burgundy and crimson decorate the countryside. For the briefest of moments nature puts on quite a show, like a peacock in the wild, and just as quickly it is all over.

The people of Morocco, and particularly the Berbers, who depend on the rain for their livelihood, have learned to live with nature's parsimony. When the rain does come, they make the best of it. These fleeting moments, celebrated in a brief explosion of colour, are the only opportunities farmers have to refill their wells and harvest the sudden sprouting of green, which they then preserve as hay for their livestock in rainless periods. Colour, thus, is synonymous with survival. If fields of desert flowers appear, the chances are that it has rained enough for the farmers to sustain their crops and feed their livestock. If not, they often end up killing their own animals in preference to watching them die slowly of starvation.

Little wonder, then, that colour is seen as a talisman against bad luck and evil spirits. In a practice dating from ancient Egypt, colour is used as a means of warding off the 'evil eye': doors and windows are painted bright blue, for instance, because it is believed that evil spirits, attracted by the colour, will linger by them and not be tempted inside the house. This tradition survives throughout the Mediterranean and particularly in Morocco. A passage in Jeffrey Becom's *Mediterranean Colour* brings these superstitions vividly to life: 'One morning I watched a man confidently painting his shop an auspicious, buoyant blue … it looked reassuring, something like the shade at the bottom of a swimming pool. With a long-handled, round bristle brush he slapped on the paint. After splashing saturated pink across his counter, he stencilled rows of Nile-green hands and lemon-yellow stars around his door until he was sure to be safe and prosperous, surrounded by his fresh bouquet of colour.'

The colour of the land also plays an important role in Morocco's culture. The tone of the local clay usually dictates the colour of the local architecture. Particularly in

the High Atlas this can create a dramatic effect. Villages set against the steep back-drop of majestic mountains are the colour of the mountains themselves. If it were not for the odd painted window or wall detail, they would be difficult to spot. The eye is confused by the absence of contrast.

Morocco is a nation where colour is used in a natural, time-proven way. Fashion does not play a role … nature does. Interestingly, the Berber sense of colour, with its love of strong, saturated shades, bears a significant resemblance to the indigenous colour sense of other mountain-dwelling peoples, such as the tribes of Tibet, Turkey and South America. It is, no doubt, a reaction to, and compensation for, their normally harsh and bleak environments. Strong colours in their weaving and their folk art are a means of capturing nature's brief explosions of colour.

Colour is part of the Moroccan way of life. Weaving, ceramics, pottery and other traditional crafts continue to use colours that have long distinguished the arts of this nation. In day-to-day life the eye is continually distracted by groupings of bright colour. *Djellabas* in oranges, lime greens, ochre yellows and hot pinks are juxtaposed with the terracotta of old city walls; in the markets, dates, melons, figs, chillies, cucumbers and enormous quantities of roses are arranged in abundant still lifes; and throughout towns and villages, walls, windows and doors are painted beautiful shades of dusty emerald green, aubergine, turquoise, rust, burnt umber, burgundy, beige, olive, cobalt blue, spring green, terracotta, lemon yellow, mustard, navy, sunset red, orange, violet, coral pink …

Colour is a constant reminder of the character of this extraordinary nation: bright, exciting, vibrant and impossible to ignore.

PREVIOUS PAGE (80)
Named after the French artist Jacques Majorelle, who used Marrakesh as his base in the 1920s, this unmistakable shade of dark blue is now referred to as 'Majorelle blue'. It was this colour that he used to paint the pots and walkways of his exceptional garden, as a foil for the greens of his collection of exotic cactuses and palms.

PREVIOUS PAGES (82–83)
The strength of Islamic art lies in the continuity of expression between the various disciplines. This mosaic of coloured glass mimics the shapes and colours that can also be found in **zillij**.

OPPOSITE

Two women dressed in the traditional manner face the wall in a small market square in Essaouira to avoid making eye contact with strangers. The white 'loomstate' cloth here complements beautifully the soft pink tones of the old town wall.

FOLLOWING PAGES (86–87)
The soft pinks and greens of this panel of **zillij** *express colours that can be found in surrounding nature at certain times of the year. The Moroccan sense of colour dates from the earliest Berber traditions. In fact, Moroccan mosaics are unique in the Islamic world because they incorporate colours such as red, pink, purple and yellow; these are shades that are not found in the mosaic decoration of other Islamic cultures.*

1	2	3	4
5	6	7	8
9	10	11	12
13	14	15	16

PHOTOS IN ORDER OF
APPEARANCE – PREVIOUS PAGES (88–89)

1 & 11

It was the Berbers, taking their cue from nature, who were responsible for the introduction of colour into all aspects of Moroccan life.

2 & 6

In sharp contrast to the bright colours of their rugs and other weaves, Berber architecture is built in the colour of the local clay. The odd whitewashed detail contrasts with the desert tones of southern Morocco.

3 & 8

The colours of the marketplace are another source of inspiration for the Moroccans' vivid sense of colour.

4

The fishing dories of Essaouira are painted in distinctive shades of blue, often with yellow highlights; a colour combination that goes back to its days as a Portuguese trading port.

5

Nature does not just contribute colour in the way of flowers and fruit. Morocco's magnificent sunsets add another dimension of colour, ranging from 'hot orange' to 'liquid gold'.

7

In the north of Morocco, white is the colour of preference for buildings, a reflection of the Mediterranean influence.

9

Bricks are often made from local clay, thus even the most elaborately constructed Islamic building reflects a tone or colour unique to the area.

10

The plaster carving skills of Moroccan artisans impart completely new dimensions to white plaster ceilings.

12 & 14

Yellow, blue and white, the colours of Portuguese majolica pottery, are also the colours used throughout the former Portuguese port of Essaouira.

13

Spices, herbal medicines, powdered dyes and cosmetic cure-alls are arranged in architectural mounds in outdoor markets throughout the country.

15

Colours in the south of Morocco tend to be softer, as if faded by the relentless Sahara sun.

16

In contrast to the bright exteriors, interiors are often dark and shaded to combat the heat.

OPPOSITE PAGE

A panel of timber carved with a traditional pattern comes to life, painted in a shade commonly known as the pale blue of the Merinid dynasty (1269–1465). Moroccan paint is quite distinctive in that it is remarkably flat, creating a sophisticated effect with bright colours.

FOLLOWING PAGES (92–93)
A Moroccan 'mise-en-scène'. A traditional indigo-blue turban, a characteristic signature of the south, a soft blue kaftan set against a yellow wall, with a doorway painted in blue to distract the **djoun** – all attest to the manner in which colour is woven into the fabric of everyday life.

4

INGREDIENTS

Design is like a language. It is often specific to a place and its overall culture. The same symbols and patterns resurface in different forms and styles and they serve as both the source and the result of creative inspiration.

ZILLIJ

THE ART

OF MOSAIC

Of all the disciplines pursued in the Islamic world to enhance and beautify buildings, the tradition of *zillij*, the creation of intricate mosaic design using hand-cut tiles, is undoubtedly the most captivating. Moroccan mosaic is compelling; it attracts the eye with a web of woven colour and mesmerizes with its intricate patterning. It is impossible not to be drawn in by it.

Islamic tradition forbids any representation of living things on the grounds that it is a decadent pagan tradition. Hence, creativity in the Islamic world has had to rely on geometry as an outlet for expression. Perhaps it is this very limitation that has given rise to such spectacular results.

Mosaic as a form of expression is almost as old as Mediterranean civilization itself. The ancient Romans went to extraordinary lengths to decorate the floors and walls of their patrician houses with tiny inlaid pieces of different-coloured stone and glass, and traces of this mosaic tradition can still be found in the remains of Morocco's own Roman city, Volubilis.

But it was the coming of Islam that really established the art form that Morocco has made its own. Spreading the word of Mohammed and absorbing, sponge-like, any worthwhile art or craft of beauty along the way, the Arab influx introduced the Persian tradition of tiled ornamentation that still adorns the domes and mausoleums of ancient cities such as Samarkand. Originally expressed purely in the blues the Persians themselves found in Chinese porcelain, this tradition was reinterpreted by the Moors into their own form of expression and from there it has grown and developed, all but obscuring its Persian origins. Moroccan *zillij* is distinguished by an extraordinary colour palette (a result of Berber influence) and by a complex mathematical geometry realized in glazed clay tiles cut into tiny individual shapes. The whole process is like a combination of abstract art and a jigsaw puzzle. As an art form it requires tremendous memory skills and a finely honed sense of order, but it also needs an artist's eye.

This distinctive art form reached its peak during the rule of the Almoravid and Almohad dynasties of the 11th–13th centuries. Some of the most famous buildings of *El Andalus*, such as the Alhambra in Granada, benefited from the complex geometric adornment that typified this period. Crusading Christians eventually brought an end to this Islamic splendour in southern Spain, but the artisans retreated to Morocco where they continued their craft.

It is extraordinary that such intricate and extremely specialized skills should have survived intact and, indeed, flourished over a period of more than a thousand years. They might easily have died out, as did the ancient tile factories of Seville that produced *azulejos*. In recent times, the continuity of this tradition has been assisted by the efforts of the present monarch, King Hassan II. Continuing the work of his father Mohammed V, he has bolstered this ancient craft by actively encouraging its use.

At the start of Hassan II's reign there were just 50 artisans remaining in Fez. But by instigating an ambitious programme of renovation at the Royal Palaces, the guild of *zillij* craftsmen has increased in number to approximately 700 today. The government has also been instrumental in establishing and supporting schools and institutions that not only study this art form but also teach it in the context of modern, practical application.

It is impossible to convey the complexity, intricacy and depth of spatial configuration in the art of *zillij*. Even with photographs it is hard to do it justice. Statistics reveal a lot more than the eye can see. First there are the raw ingredients. There are approximately 360 different shapes of cut-clay pieces, called *fourmah*, available to the composer of *zillij*, and these in turn are glazed in the traditional colours of blue, green, white, yellow and black. Red is a relatively recent addition to the colour spectrum, as are the lighter and darker shades of all the aforementioned colours. Mathematically, the number of permutations allowed by such a range of varying factors is immense. And none of it is written down. The *zillij* master, or *zlayiyyah*, commits all to memory. This is why, in the *zillij* education process, the first years are spent endlessly drawing these mathematical puzzles, so that, like language, the possible configurations coalesce into a vocabulary available for recall as necessary.

PREVIOUS PAGE (96)

This detail, taken from a wall of the main hall of the old Glaoua kasbah in Telouet, high in the Atlas Mountains, is indicative of the complexity of the combination of patterns and colours that is possible in the hands of an experienced **zlayiyyah**.

OPPOSITE

Zillij *has been called a relationship between religion and beauty. The commitment of the* **zlayiyyahs** *certainly constitutes lifelong devotion. There are over 360 different* **fourmah** *or cut tiles and each has a name and a meaning. The* **zlayiyyahs** *know every piece and*

every pattern by heart. In fact, the first six or seven years as an apprentice **zlayiyyah** *are spent endlessly drawing the multitudes of geometric configurations. The strenuous training of the memory – central to the art of* **zillij**-*making – is like the ability of the chess master to see ten or twenty moves ahead.*

Interestingly, the application of *zillij* is not governed by exact measurement of individual pieces to fit a prescribed space. Instead, the *zlayiyyah* draws on his extensive knowledge to select a geometric configuration that will work in the space.

In this way, too, the artist maintains an independence of expression, because there is not an architect in Morocco who understands this 'art form' to the degree where he can dictate a pattern exactly. Guidelines may of course be established by clients and architects, but it is ultimately the *zlayiyyah* who decides.

It has often been observed that *zillij* is 'Escher-like' in its visual construction, which is ironic since it was Escher who was, in fact, inspired by the mosaic tiling of southern Spain. One of the few Western artists to grasp the mystery and sophisticated spatial qualities of this uniquely Moorish adornment, Escher became recognized worldwide as a master of illusionary plays on repetition and perspective. He was deeply affected by visits to southern Spain where he first saw the magnificence of Moroccan mosaic in the Alhambra Palace in Granada and in the mosques of Cordoba.

But what is the relevance of *zillij* in the modern world? Is it nostalgic to keep this ancient art form alive? Aside from King Hassan II, who else has the resources to commission such finery? Considering that it takes eight craftsmen up to four months to cover twenty square metres in *zillij*, the number of working hours required to adorn a building is, in itself, mind-boggling.

Zillij is a painstaking, expensive art form, yet it remains very much relevant to modern Morocco. To reinforce tradition and national pride, the finest public buildings are adorned with *zillij* of extraordinary intricacy and complexity. Recent examples include the Hassan II Mosque in Casablanca, one of the largest and most elaborate mosques in the Islamic world.

But *zillij* is also exploited today in domestic environments. Used in the manner of an expensive rug, *zillij* is commissioned with restraint. And, ironically, a restrained use of this art serves to highlight its beauty. By making it more precious the tradition also redefines its own economic relevance. Being expensive means that it is used in a more minimal and, thus, modern manner.

OPPOSITE
An old house in the Marrakesh **medina** *features a cut-tile mosaic, unusual in its strict use of blue and white. The enormous variety in the art of Moroccan ceramics can be attributed to patterns that* *have perhaps been repeated by 28 successive generations of* **zlayiyyahs**.

FOLLOWING PAGES (102–103)
Morocco's leading architects and designers are attempting to interpret **zillij** *in a modern* *manner.* **Zillij** *panels are now used more in the manner of a beautiful rug on a plain floor. In this way, the art form is preserved and updated. All the patterns on the following two pages are examples of* **zillij** *in contemporary applications.*

MOROCCAN

POTTERY

The bright colours and simple, elegant shapes of Morocco's pottery are part of a tradition that started more than 2000 years ago. Making vessels and objects from clay is known to date back as far as the Neolithic period and many designs in Moroccan pottery made today originated in the 6th century BC.

Morocco's pottery provides a direct, recognizable link with the Mediterranean origins of civilization. Clay vessels made in the Rif area look almost exactly the same as ancient Carthaginian pots. Similarly, other pieces closely resemble the terracotta vessels of ancient Rome. Virtually all of Mediterranean history is reflected in the extensive range of clay handiwork made by village potters throughout Morocco.

Pottery, like many of Morocco's art and craft traditions, has, over time, benefited from complex, overlapping influences, but one aspect has remained constant: throughout history, 'utility' has always been the guiding principle in pottery production. Simplicity in form and decoration stems from the fact that these pieces were, and still are, made to be used. It also explains why so few old pieces have survived.

The most enduring influence on Moroccan pottery came during the long period of cultural interaction with the Andalusian emirates of Granada and Seville. For hundreds of years, the two neighbouring Islamic communities, separated by the Strait of Gibraltar, exchanged ideas and techniques in all the different crafts. Ceramics (glazed and fired clay vessels) were deemed of particular importance, as is illustrated in a tale about Youssef Bin Tachfine, Almoravid sultan and founder of Marrakesh. Having lost the city of Toledo to the Christians, the Emirs of Granada and Seville asked Sultan Youssef Bin Tachfine for help. The Berber ruler and his fierce, veiled warriors crossed the Strait and pushed the Christians back to the north. His price for this good deed was a request for the craftsmen responsible for the plates he had so admired at a banquet given in his honour in Andalusia. Not long after, a family of ceramists took up residence in Marrakesh. Perhaps the Emir of Granada came to wish he had used his everyday 'flatware' on that one occasion.

The time of the Almoravids and Almohads was a golden age that ended with the *Reconquista*. King Ferdinand and Queen Isabella's expulsion of all Jews and Muslims

and the beginning of the treacherous 'Spanish Inquisition' put a swift and tragic end to this cultural flowering in southern Spain.

The only winner was the sultanate of Morocco, which gained all the exiled craftsmen, in the same way that, a century later, Holland and England would benefit from the persecution of Huguenot craftsmen by the French. Morocco's new residents were craftsmen who had dedicated their lives to learning a trade. Yet their achievements never again reached the intensity of the time when Islam still dominated both sides of the Strait.

Meanwhile, life in the Berber village went on regardless. Unlike weaving and embroidery, which are done by the women, pottery and ceramics are practised by the men. It is said in Berber village folklore that there are only two worthy pursuits for a man – waging war and making pottery. Besides a genuine regard for function, male potters are concerned with their craft not becoming too effeminate. Thus, decoration and form are consciously pared down.

Berber pottery is meant to distract the 'evil eye'. This, combined with the utilitarian role of pottery, has elevated its status. Shards of pots are found in cemeteries because they allegedly protect the dead from evil spirits. In certain parts of Morocco, potters still produce their entire repertoire in miniature to allow these pieces to be hung on the wall to provide further protection from evil spirits.

Pottery reflects the rural Berber tradition, whereas its more colourful and shiny counterpart, ceramics, is more urban and Islamic. The painted, glazed ceramics used for tableware are the most dramatic. Traditionally, the colours of Moroccan ceramics are green, yellow and brown. Interestingly, cobalt or Majorelle blue, although so vividly associated with Morocco, wasn't introduced until 1853 by Fassi merchants living in England.

Born of necessity and fired with a deep-seated spirituality, Morocco's pottery and ceramics have survived several millennia of turbulent events and history to emerge intact as a strong reminder of the depth and beauty of the nation's culture.

PREVIOUS PAGE (104)

The Moroccan tradition of making vessels in clay continues a process of evolution with the introduction of contemporary design influences to an ancient medium. This large platter, decorated with simple concentric stripes of cobalt blue, is an interesting example of 'modern' Moroccan pottery.

PREVIOUS PAGES (106–107)

The most significant change in Moroccan ceramics in recent times has been the shift in the direction of a less decorative repertoire of plates, bowls and other items. The uneven finish and irregular shape of these brightly coloured vessels turn them into quite an enticing temptation for Western visitors.

OPPOSITE

A vase, designed in the same manner as the platter on page 104, continues the successful marriage of contemporary design and traditional craft. The spiral pattern shown here was most probably inspired by the 'immortality spiral' that often adorns the silver discs of traditional Berber necklaces.

1	2	3	4	5	6
7	8	9	10	11	12
13	14	15	16	17	18

PHOTOS IN ORDER OF
APPEARANCE – PREVIOUS PAGES (110–111)

1 & 18

These were conceived as water jugs – polychrome designs with floral motifs on white background. Early 20th century, Fez.

2 & 17

Large pots without lids, traditionally used as vases.

3 & 4

Vases without handles and a more stylized (i.e. stricter) decoration reveal contemporary influences in traditional Moroccan pottery.

5

Many ceramic items were originally designed for serving a specific kind of food. Amongst the most popular were soup tureens – deep dishes with a lid.

6 & 13

Smaller pots decorated in typical Fez patterns are made more in response to recent decorative demands than for any particular traditional purpose.

7

A water cooling pot, now largely made only for decorative purposes.

8

Brown, derived from manganese, is one of the traditional colours of Moroccan pottery. The others are yellow and green. Red and blue were, historically speaking, relatively recent additions.

9, 11 & 15

Diverse in shape, these three pieces are most probably from Safi as opposed to Fez. Safi ceramics are distinguished by simpler, bolder, predominantly geometric motifs.

10

The segmented (in bands) manner of decoration reflects traditional pottery's relationship to the land. A pot is decorated in the way one would plough a field – in strips.

12

The softness of the colours and the intricacy of the decoration suggest that this piece from the pottery guilds of Fez dates back a century, although it is difficult to be certain.

14

Constellations of four-petalled flowers outlined in brown, set in a green background – an early 20th-century design from Fez.

16

Lozenge-shape geometrics and a particularly lustrous glaze distinguish the ceramics of Safi from those of other regions.

Opposite page

Brightly coloured pottery is more associated with the Arabic traditions of Morocco's cities than the more earthy traditions of the Berber village. Simple unadorned plates are a recent response to Western consumer demands. Made in the same manner and method as the crockery that distinguished Moroccan culture at its 12th-century zenith, the pottery's imperfections have the appeal of the handmade.

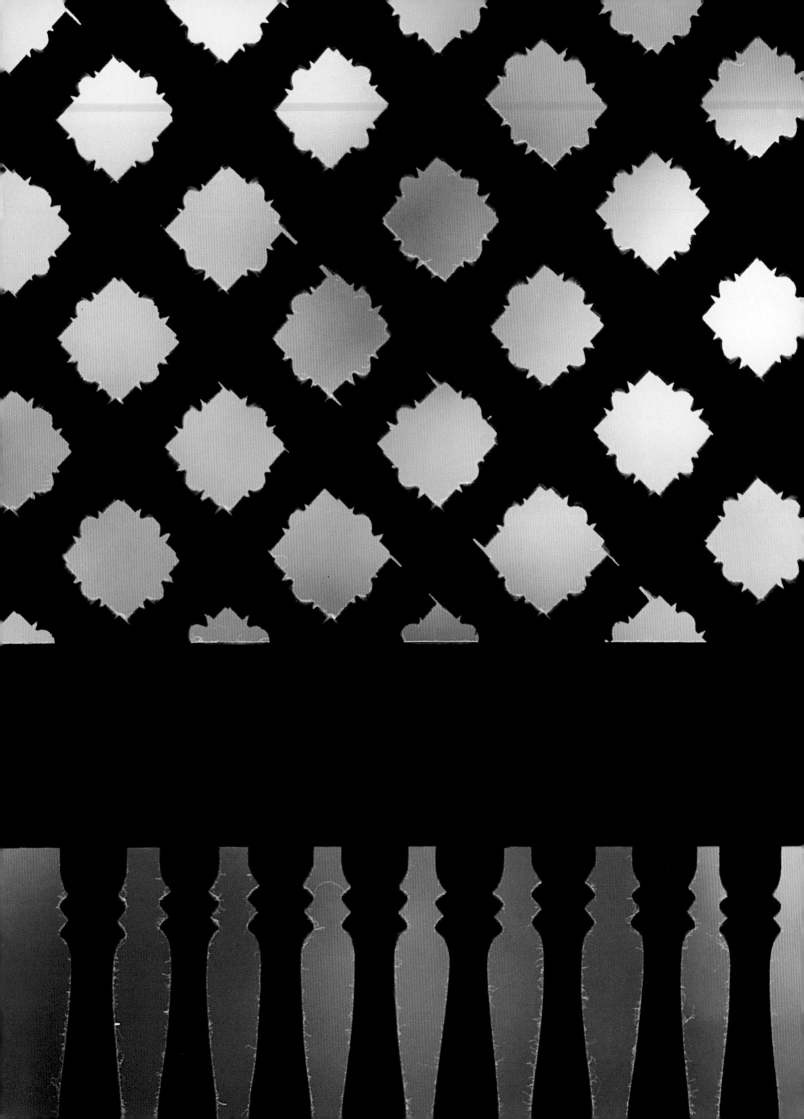

AND

MOROCCAN
WOODWORK

The one creative tradition entirely unique to Morocco among Islamic states in Africa is woodwork. Timber, particularly cedar, is reasonably abundant in the Middle Atlas region and this availability has driven a craft tradition that is responsible for some intricately monumental work, particularly in the cities of Fez, Marrakesh, Essaouira, Tetouan and Meknès. Entirely the preserve of men, the profession of woodworking has long been organized along the lines of corporations or guilds with strict codes and rules to control working practices. Close-knit communities, these guilds often pass membership through families from generation to generation. Sons are most likely to be the apprentices and they in turn become *maallems* and teach their sons.

The most magnificent expression of the woodworker's skills, as with most Moroccan artisan traditions, is reserved for the mosques and *medersas* (seminaries where holy men learn the Koran) and for the palaces of the king. And in these palaces, mosques and universities, the most impressive feature is often the door. Doors play a big role in Moroccan architecture. Throughout the country, doors of massive proportions with elaborate detailing stand impressively against thick red mud or white stucco walls. Decorated with an exquisitely carved ornamental vocabulary that includes calligraphy, geometrical motifs and the ubiquitous Berber talismanic images, these elaborate portals are the result of much preparation and long fore-thought. As with the art of *zillij*, the *maallem* chooses his design from a vast array of options that he has committed to memory and, once decided upon, the selected design is drawn and cut into a paper stencil. It is then realized using various techniques, including incising, inlay, pyro-engraving, stamping and painting – though, generally speaking, painting is primarily reserved for interiors and is rarely used on doors. The latter are exposed to the elements and, being made of cedar, require little maintenance so long as they are dried properly before cutting.

Hands of Fatima, fibulas, ancient triangular symbols of fertility and fecundity, geo-metric star patterns of eight, twelve or sixteen points, and entire necklaces or chokers are often carved onto doors for protection against the *djoun* or evil spirits. This is particularly true of the doors to the *agadir*, a granary built like a fortress on top of a hill or mountain, protected by a steep path providing limited access and an imposingly massive door. In times of fierce tribal warfare, not so long ago (earlier this century, in fact), these citadel-like structures with their strongroom doors were the only means by which to protect lives, possessions and food from marauding tribes.

Another application of the woodworker's skill that is highly characteristic of Islamic countries is the ornate screens, formed by a series of turned wooden bobbins glued or nailed into a grid, known as *moushrabiyas*. Beautifully geometric in appearance, with octagonal or star-shaped openings, *moushrabiyas* derive from Muslim society's tradition of keeping the women of the household hidden from view. In accordance with Islamic law they do not mingle with men in places of worship or in reception rooms. Usually installed in the upper galleries or patios of private homes, these screens allow the women of the household to move about and observe the goings-on without themselves being seen. Until recent times, women were discouraged from leaving the domestic domain, a sentiment embodied in the old Moroccan proverb: 'There is no blessing in a woman who travels and there is no blessing in a man who does not travel.' Morocco today, however, is seen as a progressive Islamic state and *moushrabiyas*, although still produced by the woodworking guilds, are now largely commissioned for their decorative beauty. Still, the origins of this discipline add to the mystery of Moroccan architecture and its interiors. The most important thing is that the skill to make these complex geometric screens has survived.

The same can be said of other items in the Moroccan woodworker's repertoire. In the past, the ornate timber detailing that went into a rifle butt was symbolic of the lofty importance that Moroccan society attached to the ability to wage war. Rifle and horseback warfare, majestic as it is, has gone, but the same skills are today being used in the production of domestic furniture for both local and foreign consumption. Exquisitely carved and painted tea tables, marriage chairs, beautifully decorated chests, sugar hammers for the preparation of traditional mint tea, ceremonial Koran holders and all manner of finely detailed shelves and cupboards acknowledge and continue the Moroccan woodworking tradition.

PREVIOUS PAGE (114)
Ornamental screens were originally devised to separate the men from the women. Their function is now more decorative.

OPPOSITE
Woodwork, another form of artistic expression that has achieved extraordinary levels *of beauty in Morocco, is used mainly for architecture, and of all the architectural details the door is probably the feature that is most characteristic of Moroccan woodwork.*

FOLLOWING PAGES (118–119)
In addition to the familiar appearance of linked wooden *bobbins, as illustrated on page 114, **moushrabiyas** can also be more densely designed with star-shaped or octagonal openings cut out of a large flat piece of wood, as is the case with the panel photographed here. In common with all other Islamic art forms, the design is made up of geometric patterns.*

"No trees anywhere,

nothing but these carpets of flowers;

as far as the view extends,

incomparable patterns on the plain;

but the expression, 'a carpet of flowers',

has been so abused in application to ordinary meadows

that it has lost the force needed for description here:

zones absolutely pink with large mallows;

marblings white as snow, which are masses of daisies;

streaks of magnificent yellow, which are trails of buttercups.

Never, in any garden, in any artificial English flower bed,

have I seen such a luxuriance of flowers,

such a packed grouping of the same kinds,

giving together such vivid colours."

Pierre Loti
Morocco, 1889

THE
BARAKA

OF THE

WEAVER'S
MAGIC

By the late 19th century Orientalism was a well-established phenomenon in Europe. 'The Orient' did not refer to Japan and China, but rather to the Islamic world of Turkey, Egypt, the Middle East and parts of North Africa. Drawn on by the allure of the exotic, the traveller found in the *Maghreb El Aqsa*, 'the land furthest west', a whole other world of colour and sensuality. Artists such as Delacroix and Matisse were heavily influenced by the colour of Moroccan life. Matisse, who spent several years there, drew inspiration and techniques from Moroccan textiles. Looking back on his career, he wrote in 1947 that 'revelation thus came to me from the "Orient".'

Weaving is perhaps the greatest of Moroccan artistic traditions; it is also one of the oldest. When the Berbers first inhabited the plains and mountains of the Atlas around 1500 BC, they are thought to have brought rudimentary weaving skills with them. Technical improvements came with commerce. Shawls, blankets, rugs and tents were traded with the Africans of Mali, Senegal and Nigeria and the Arabs from the east, and from the Phoenicians the Berbers learned more about the art of dyeing. The process was accelerated by the spread of Islam in the 7th century. United by a single religion, North Africa became one huge marketplace for the woollen cloths, brocades and silks woven in Morocco. Religious influence also brought new symbols and motifs, especially in the form of the rigorous geometries that distinguish Islamic art. Portuguese and Arab ledgers from the first sultanate confirm the new status of Moroccan weaves as currency – textiles had become an integral part of the economy.

Profit, however, was not the village weaver's sole motive. Rugs and carpets are said to contain *baraka*, or 'beneficent psychic powers'. Vibrant colours are used to offset the darkness of dimly lit rooms, but the actual motifs are related largely to superstition. The most common of these is the hand of Fatima, used to ward off the 'evil eye' and the *djoun*. Other motifs are believed to have the power to draw and then dissipate evil in the six directions of the Berber universe. Interestingly, despite centuries of Islamic influence and the traditional prohibition on figurative representation, tribal weaving still incorporates the Berber vocabulary of animist symbols, albeit in a disciplined, geometric form.

In rural areas, weaving still follows the rhythm of village life. The men of the village tend the sheep while the women do the weaving, besides carrying out the preparatory steps such as washing, spinning and dyeing. For these women, who sing together and tell tales of superstition as they work, weaving is a skill that can increase their 'dowry price' substantially. Stylistically, the rugs of these villages share an earthy simplicity and graphic boldness, despite the fact that the weavers may use entirely different colours and motifs. To the collector or connoisseur of Moroccan textiles, these are the most valuable. Largely flat-woven like Turkish *kilims*, they are often embellished with symmetrical knots. Colour is used in strong bands across the rug. In addition, or sometimes instead, Moroccan *kilims* feature symbols arranged in bands, as if to mimic the ubiquitous stripe. Broadly speaking, the classic flat stripes woven predominantly in the south are referred to as *Glaoua*, a term derived from the name of the most powerful Berber tribe in the south of Morocco.

The urban weaving tradition, most probably growing out of the influx of craftsmen after the fall of Granada in 1492, is responsible for an entirely different product. The style of the rugs and carpets produced in Morocco's cities is inspired by those of Turkey and Persia, from which the composition, motifs and colours are borrowed. Often knotted as opposed to flat-woven, these more sumptuous but less original designs are distinguished by the symmetrical placement of their geometric and floral motifs, their clearly defined borders and their quite pronounced dominant colour, the most popular of which is red.

Whether of rural or urban origin, Moroccan rugs are the product of a unique country and people, whose sense of beauty was poignantly celebrated by Delacroix: 'They are closer to nature in a thousand ways, their dress, the form of their shoes. And so beauty has a share in everything they make. As for us in our corsets, our tight shoes, our ridiculous pinching shoes, we are pitiful.'

PREVIOUS PAGE (122)
Moroccan tribal textiles are some of the most dazzling and impressive in Africa and are perhaps the most ancient, possibly dating from around 1500 BC when the Berbers first settled in North Africa.

PREVIOUS PAGES (124–125)
The single most captivating feature of Moroccan weaving would have to be the brilliant use of colour. As Gauguin wrote: 'You painters who clamour for a colour technique, study these carpets and they will tell you all you want to know … From this kind of colour, definite in its inherent charm yet indefinite as an indication of objects perceived in nature, there arises a disconcerting question: What can that possibly mean? And I say, what does it matter?'

OPPOSITE
Rug production in Morocco is highly regionalized in terms of styles and influences. Rural production in villages tends to concentrate on flat weaves of lattice patterns and stripes. The plainest, simplest and, therefore, in a modern sense, the most graphic rugs tend to come from the remotest villages of the High Atlas region.

5

VIRTUOSI

In music, in art, in almost every human creative endeavour, there are always people who stand out, people whose achievements warrant focus and attention. They often establish new directions and create pioneering approaches; they are leaders – they are the virtuosi in their chosen field of expertise.

THE

ARCHITECTURE

OF

CHARLES

BOCCARA

Charles Boccara is an out-and-out enthusiast. He runs around his own buildings, showing off his ideas, inspirations and preferences, eager to get to the next space, eager to explain, with all hands, arms and feet engaged, the art that he has chosen to dedicate his life to.

Architecture is clearly not just his job, but also his passion. Apart from producing some of the most beautiful buildings in Morocco, he is also immensely prolific. As he says, he wants to 'work and work' because it is not about making the perfect building, it is about continually striving to do so. For him, practice is the key – a writer must write, an architect must build. Churchill coined this sentiment perfectly when he said, 'Perfection is spelled p.a.r.a.l.y.s.i.s.'

Characterized by the clever creation of open yet predominantly private spaces and the enthusiastic patronage of Moroccan craft traditions, Boccara's work is peppered with intricately tiled courtyards, elaborately constructed bathrooms, expansive ceilings decorated with traditional colours and finishes and other examples of rich and seductive detailing. His work is so closely aligned with the spirit and atmosphere of Morocco that one tends to forget he is not a Moroccan native.

Tunisian-born and Paris-trained, Charles Boccara is nicknamed 'the master' for his singular life-long devotion to the development of an appropriate modern architecture for Morocco. Drawing on Moroccan tradition, particularly the architecture of the Almoravid and Almohad dynasties of the 11th–13th centuries, his buildings convey a sense of belonging whilst maintaining an unquestionably modern signature. Endowed with the culture of the region, they are not sentimental or nostalgic, nor do they expect the owner/occupier to sacrifice Western standards of living.

Of all his projects, one of the most fascinating and photogenic is Douar Abiad, a small residential oasis in Marrakesh's Palmerai. Situated on a dusty road running through the middle of the palm grove, Douar Abiad is a mud-walled compound distinguished by the majestic twin towers that define the entry. Within the walls of the compound, four houses are set in a plush oasis of exotic flowers and abundant green vegetation. Built looking inwards to their own courtyard, with mosaic tiled swimming pools and fountains, each house is literally an oasis within an oasis: a private retreat representing the perfect synthesis of traditional style and powerful modernity.

Unlike many, Boccara is not an architect to lose sleep over the choice of a door-knob. Based in Marrakesh, he has the advantage of working in a place that still has the most precious of all things to offer an architect: demand for new architecture. His work does not consist of converting small inner-city apartments by moving a wall here and a sink there. He builds. And he builds from scratch; and that is why he is so animated and enthusiastic about living and working in Morocco. It offers the ultimate for any enthusiast, namely: opportunity.

But he is not a workaholic. He is as driven as any architect, just not at lunchtime. In step with the quality of life that a place like Marrakesh can still provide, he enjoys the things that make life pleasant – food, drink, conversation … beauty. His capacity for *joie de vivre* comes through in his buildings. Perhaps the best example of all is his own home. Set in the exotic surroundings of the Marrakesh Palmerai, he has created a verdant retreat that provides, in true Arabic style, a haven from the bustle, dust and heat of Marrakesh city life. He describes it not as a house, but as a collection of houses that, in turn, have their own houses. What he means by this is not immediately apparent. And that seems to be part of the idea. Boccara loves mystery; surprise and a degree of obscurity are features he has striven to make part of his house and garden. His estate has something of the spirit of the *medina*, with all its little unexpected, self-

PREVIOUS PAGE (130)
*Twin towers mark the entrance to Douar Abiad, a small group of contemporary houses built within a single walled compound on the outskirts of Marrakesh. Rendered in the traditional mud, the towers mimic the monolithic nature of the great Berber **ksour** and **kasbahs** that are found on the fringes of the Sahara.*

PREVIOUS PAGES (132–133)
*Built around an internal court-yard or **riyadh**, defined on three sides by wings of the house and on the fourth by a small walled garden, these houses all follow the strict and primary principle of traditional Moroccan houses. A distinct signature of all the houses is the abundant use of **zillij** on the floors.*

OPPOSITE
*An outdoor corridor running adjacent to the main living area doubles as a place to sit. Floor-to-ceiling curtains keep out the sun during the hotter months. Each house is distin-guished by a certain number of hidden and unexpected spaces, as seen here by the view through the archway leading to another hidden **riyadh** or courtyard.*

FOLLOWING PAGES (136–137)
*One house is distinguished by an elaborate tower (housing a small children's bedroom) which overlooks the swimming pool. The view from the tower dis-torts the many layers of decora-tive **zillij** used along the stairs, becoming an almost abstract*

collage of different colours, patterns and scales. The blue and brown tiles in the fore-ground actually constitute the sides of the stairs leading up to the tower.

FOLLOWING PAGE (138)
In sharp contrast to the bright colour and light that dominate it during the day, the living room in one of the houses becomes quite warm and cosy at night – a reflection, no doubt, of the extremes of a desert culture. Colours and tones of interiors in southern Morocco still mimic the ambience of tents. Following an old, estab-lished Moroccan tradition, living rooms tend to be long and narrow, usually with a rather impressive fireplace at one end.

"Nowhere in the Arab world has the art of Islamic architecture reached the point of sophistication it has in Morocco, a country which has developed its own unique architectural vocabulary and language. El Andalus was not lamented here – it was reinstated."

Salma Samar Damluji
Zillij: The Art of Moroccan Ceramics, 1992

1	2	3	4	5	6
7	8	9	10	11	12
13	14	15	16	17	18

PHOTOS IN ORDER OF
APPEARANCE – PREVIOUS PAGES (140–141)

1 & 15

Hanging from oleander branch panelled ceilings, plaster lamps with coloured glass inserts are a contemporary interpretation of traditional mosque lanterns.

2 & 17

In form and particularly in detail Charles Boccara's buildings borrow from Mauresque architecture and the Berber 'mud castles'.

3, 10 & 18

Within architecture of unquestionably modern design, Charles Boccara makes use, wherever possible, of traditional crafts and finishes. Ceilings are panelled with oleander branches and then painted in vivid geometric patterns.

4

Old doors, or new ones constructed in the manner of traditional Moroccan doors, add character and a sense of appropriateness to the architecture.

5

Peering out of the top of a lush palm-tree oasis, the roof of a bathroom is mimicked by the canopy on a chimney. These sculptural touches add mystery, charm and fun to the architecture.

6

A cut-out in the gate towers of the entrance combines traditional 'flat brick' masonry with an evocative shape.

7

*A **zillij**-tiled courtyard divides the front door and the entrance to the house. It is typical of Boccara's penchant for creating small, surprising spaces.*

8

*A dining room fireplace combines the craft tradition of **zillij** with the forms of classical Egyptian architecture.*

9

Windows as well as doorways are often placed in the manner one would frame a picture.

11

*An Islamic archway frames the exotic brick masonry of one of the bathrooms and the tub is finished in **tadlekt**.*

12

Gardens are another impressive aspect of Boccara's domestic architecture. They envelop and frame the building like verdant packaging.

13

*Floors are exquisite examples of detailing. White marble, **zillij** and **tadlekt** are combined like a modern Moroccan still life.*

14

A small cut-out behind a swimming pool is another example of a penchant for creating spaces that have no direct function other than to add to the experience of the architecture.

16

*A balcony leading off a main bedroom is a contemporary composition of Moroccan ingredients. **Moushrabiya** is used for the railing, mud render for the walls and oleander branch panelling for the ceilings.*

Opposite

Character, authenticity, imagination and a certain sense of fun inform the architecture of Charles Boccara. The exterior of this bathroom (the interior of which is featured on pages 144–145) is built as a freestanding pavilion. The idea of a bathroom with its own terrace is typical of Boccara's belief that spaces should, in turn, have their own spaces.

contained spaces. And it has something of the maze-like qualities of the old city centre. Every room, every space leads to other spaces, some obvious, some obscure.

Boccara's own house contains numerous allusions to the 'golden age' of Islamic culture in Morocco. Strong historical reference is part of his distinctive signature. As one of the key design figures leading Morocco into the next century, Boccara is concerned with maintaining continuity – cultural continuity.

His house is endowed with the historical qualities of Islamic architecture. There is the symmetry, the courtyard and the correct detailing in terms of style and ingredients: a thoroughly modern house with a traditional allocation of space; a family home as well as an exquisite building. It is quite a mix. Rarely does a building have so many different personalities simultaneously and so successfully. Boccara has brought the ingredients of Moroccan culture into the 20th century without losing the very quality – the sense of the exotic and the mysterious – that has always been Marrakesh's appeal.

Mystery, surprise, even folly are qualities that, in Boccara's opinion, Western architects have been prepared to give up all too readily. 'What a pity,' he says, for he is convinced that 'getting lost' is one of the real pleasures of a house – even if it has no clear rationale or function: such things are, sadly, all too often left out of the equation. The resulting buildings have nothing to offer beyond what is immediately understood. Boccara laments the loss of new architecture's ability to be mysterious.

Boccara's descriptions of his own work don't involve tedious facts and statistics; rather, he speaks, always passionately and with animation, about notions and ideas of a more philosophical nature. They reveal a lot about the man and a lot about his architecture. He loves the idea, for instance, of creating a path along the orchid pool and then never using it, choosing instead to walk next to the path. He likes the idea of

PREVIOUS PAGES (144–145)
*Inspired by the domed structure of the traditional Moroccan **hammam** (steam room), the bathrooms feature soaring ceilings capped by a dome, all built in a dazzling display of the skills of the local brick masons. Natural light makes its way in through round holes which would have originally been glazed with bottle bottoms. The exterior of this particular bathroom can be seen on page 143.*

OPPOSITE
Born in Tunis, brought up in Morocco and trained at the Ecole des Beaux-Arts in Paris, architect Charles Boccara chose to work in Morocco because the language of building is still nourished by strong traditions – traditions, both abstracted and literal, that he used for his own house. The veranda, leading off the main living area, reveals his fondness for classical Egyptian architecture.

FOLLOWING PAGES (148–149)
Facing in the opposite direction to the veranda depicted on page 147, this wing of Boccara's own house, which includes the kitchen, a small breakfast room and a study, looks out onto an expansive orchid pool. At certain times of the day the noise generated by all the resident frogs can be genuinely deafening. Charles Boccara loves it. The pool, he says, 'is teeming with life'.

providing a hidden courtyard for the bathroom because it makes the space less finite. Being in the bathroom then automatically becomes less restrictive since other options exist, even if they are not used. In our conversation he made the analogy with houses that have an attic, a space that is hardly ever visited yet contains the soul and mystery of the house and its occupants. It is a fascinating and refreshing way to think about architecture. He is also not a great fan of rationalizing everything. If he chooses to adorn the stone fireplace in his daughter's bedroom with elephants, he doesn't feel particularly compelled to justify his decision. His design has an element of playfulness and spontaneity. Yet at the same time, it doesn't stray too far from its cultural roots.

Surrounded by a couple of hectares of palm grove set inside a walled compound, Boccara's own house evokes the feeling of Morocco's glorious *kasbahs*. He has borrowed extensively from the glorious age of Morocco's Almoravid and Almohad dynasties, utilizing the scale and form of this period and making generous use of the craft traditions that have continued unbroken to this day. From the massive carved timber gates of the entrance and the distinctive green tiled roof, typical of the finest palaces of *El Andalus*, to the exquisite mosaic tiling of the swimming pool, the house recreates and redefines all the great traditions of Moroccan culture.

OPPOSITE

*The main living room is distinguished by a ceiling height of a staggering 7 metres (23 feet). As Boccara says, 'If I conceive a marvellous room with a very high ceiling, then why not enhance its presence with beautiful woodwork? These decorative crafts still exist in Morocco, so why not use them?' The room also features a traditional Moroccan chandelier, a **tadlekt** floor, a superb fireplace and, as can be expected in an architect's house, the ubiquitous Eames chairs.*

FOLLOWING PAGE (152)

One place where all his ideas and inspirations come together beautifully is the bathroom. Charles Boccara does great bathrooms, perhaps better than anyone else. He is at heart a romantic and he is, as he says,

*'enchanted by memories of the past'. He likes to utilize elements like old wooden doors, antique marble washbasins, even plumbing fixtures from the 1920s. In light of the decorative impact of the **zillij** he uses on the walls and floor, it is understandable why these creations are so enchanting.*

FOLLOWING PAGE (153)

The kitchen is another superb example of his ability to combine modernity with the charm of history. An impressive traditional vaulted ceiling, finished in the signature masonry style of Moroccan Islamic architecture, is juxtaposed with the simplest of tables and some bentwood chairs. The basin, carved from a magnificent chunk of black and white marble, becomes the type of decorative focal point that

Boccara likes. In his own words: 'I am fond of the juxtaposition of simplicity in volume and rich articulation in the detailing, something that is still possible in Morocco.'

FOLLOWING PAGE (154)

*The veranda that leads directly from the living room is exemplary of the house's simplicity and modernity. The decoration again reinforces Boccara's overall approach of combining simple spaces with rich articulation and detailing. The pillars, quite neo-classical in inspiration, are constructed of typical flat Moroccan bricks, whereas the spaces left by stacking are then filled with mortar. The floors are embellished with **zillij** and the balcony balustrades are a typical example of **moushrabiya**.*

"They are closer to nature in a thousand ways, their dress, the form of their shoes. And so beauty has a share in everything they make. As for us in our corsets, our tight shoes, our ridiculously pinching shoes, we are pitiful."

Eugène Delacroix

ACKNOWLEDGMENTS

This book would never have been produced without the guidance and assistance of **Chris Lawrence** *and his family. Without their enthusiasm for Morocco and the wonderful insider's knowledge that they have gained through their business 'Best of Morocco', I doubt I would have seen the Morocco that so inspired me to do a book. Their experience of organizing and developing fashion and film 'shoots' as well as their specialization in off-the-beaten-track tours of Morocco allowed me to 'fast track' the normally time-consuming process of research and location hunting, and the 'on location' assistance provided by* **Max Lawrence** *ensured that we were able, as a team, to work at an incredibly productive speed.*

Special thanks go to **Samantha Todhunter**, *who not only lent her creative eye to many of the 'shoots' we were doing, but who was also responsible for getting me to Morocco in the first place. Her instinct for making the right contacts proved to be, as always, 'spot on'.*

I was also extremely lucky to meet **Meryanne Loum Martin**, *the proprietress of Dar Tamsna, one of the Palmerai's most beautiful villas. Although she has had an estate in Marrakesh for the better part of a decade, her interest in and fascination with Morocco is still fresh and inspirational. From her I learned much more about Morocco's craft traditions, in a hands-on manner, than I would have working only from books, and her input added to the material of this book.*

Finally, the efforts of the people behind the scenes must be mentioned: **Jan Heinen** *at* **Kader Design** *and the team at* **Lifoka Reprographics** *and* **Zijderveld Studio**. *I must also extend my warmest thanks once more to my friend and collaborator,* **Willem Rethmeier**, *without whom I could not have produced this book.*

PHOTOGRAPHY CREDITS

First and foremost, the photography in this book would not have been possible without the tireless dedication of Willem Rethmeier. All photographs are by him, with the exception of pp. 64, 69, 70, 73, 75, 82–83, 88–89, 92–93, for which thanks to Chris Lawrence.

BIBLIOGRAPHY

BIDWELL, MARGARET AND ROBIN. 1992. *Morocco: The Traveller's Companion*. London.

DENNIS, LANDT AND LISL. 1992. *Living in Morocco*. London.

ELLINGHAM, MARK, SHAUN MCVEIGH, AND DON GRISBROOK. 1993. *Morocco: The Rough Guide*. London.

HEDGECOE, JOHN, AND SALMA SAMAR DAMLUJI. 1992. *Zillij: The Art of Moroccan Ceramics*. Reading.

INGRAM, JIM. 1952. *A Land of Mud Castles*. London.

JEREB, JAMES F. 1995. *Arts and Crafts of Morocco*. London.

MAXWELL, GAVIN. 1966. *Lords of the Atlas*. London.

PACCARD, ANDRÉ. 1979. *Traditional Islamic Craft in Moroccan Architecture*. St Jorioz.

PICKERING, BROOKE, W. RUSSEL PICKERING, AND RALPH S. YOHE. 1994. *Moroccan Carpets*. London.

TILES

AND TAJINE

Throughout the Islamic world, clay tiles have been used for walls, floors and courtyards for more than a thousand years. In Morocco the range of tiles is particularly varied. Among the most attractive and least expensive are the simple, square clay tiles distinguished by their flat, matte-like finish. Sealed but not glazed, they have the slightly uneven signature of a handmade product and they are produced with the flair for colour for which Morocco is renowned. The earthenware **tajine** *is a typically Moroccan vessel used to prepare and serve stews served on a bed of* **couscous.**

Tiles available from Fired Earth Tel. 44 171 221 4825

Tajine *available from Habitat
Tel. 44 171 631 3880*

MAJORELLE

BLUE

Jacques Majorelle was a French artist who lived in Marrakesh in the 1920s and 1930s. His best-known legacy is not, however, his paintings but his garden. Restored to its former glory by fashion designer Yves Saint Laurent, Jardin Majorelle is a big tourist draw. All the pots, walkways, fountains and other 'architecture' that sit among an extra-ordinary collection of cactuses, palms, bamboo and other exotic flora are painted a distinct shade of blue now commonly referred to as 'Majorelle blue'. By trial and error you could eventually mix this colour yourself; or you could just buy a pot of 'Blue Kasbah' from the Kasbah, a large Moroccan emporium situated in the heart of London's Covent Garden.

Available from the Kasbah Tel. 44 171 240 3538

MONOCHROME

POTTERY

Plain pottery in bright colours, distinguished by beautiful glazed shades of green, blue and yellow, are the product of an urban tradition. Made in the major ceramic centres of Fez, Meknès, Marrakesh and Safi, this enamelled ware originates from the time when the **tallayahs,** *the artisans who specialize in glazed tableware, produced all the plates, bowls, platters, etc for all classes of people in the cities. The irregular handmade 'character' and beautiful, bright, plain colours have found a new and very appreciative audience in the Western world. Interestingly, the strong demand for this type of pottery for export has reawakened an interest among Moroccans as well.*

*Selection of bowls and plates available from Habitat
Tel. 44 171 631 3880*

OLD TIN

TEA CONTAINERS

The serving of tea, a long-standing Arabic tradition, was until recently quite an elaborate process, requiring an extraordinary assortment of tools and containers. Essential to the whole process was a hammer for crushing sugar crystal into manageable lumps, a container to hold the leaves of fresh mint, a smaller version to hold the tea and a small open cup to hold the crystals of sugar. Many old containers, hammers and the like end up in the Marrakesh **souks.** *The oval containers in particular can be very attractive in new guises. Short of visiting the* **souks** *of Marrakesh, your best bet is to ask 'Best of Morocco'*

Best of Morocco Tel. 44 1380 828533

MODERN

PLATTER AND PLATE

The main concern of the village potter in Morocco has always been function. Very few pieces of pottery were ever made for decoration. Plates, platters, bowls and pots were made to be used. Not much has changed. Simplicity and utility are still the guiding principles of the village potter. Therefore the introduction of strong, simple graphics is very much in keeping with tradition and in no way compromises the village potter's old values. Small wonder, then, that Morocco's pottery appears to be so modern. It is simply a case of 'form follows function', or perhaps more accurately, 'form follows culture'.

Available from
Designers Guild Tel. 44 171 351 5775
Ikea Tel. 44 181 208 5600

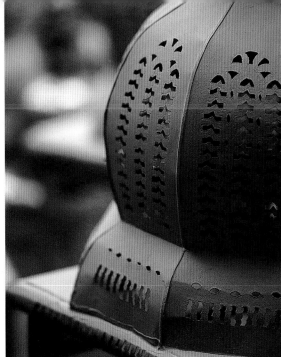

DECORATIVE

LANTERN

In the land of the 'Thousand and One Nights' it is not surprising to find an extraordinary selection of candle-lit lanterns. The charm and romance of lantern light are without equal. Large numbers of lanterns are used to light garden paths, the periphery of swimming pools and any outdoor areas where people may choose to dine. The magic of these settings is not lost on the Western visitor, judging from the number of tourists that depart Morocco with a lantern. Styles vary from simple perforated tin constructions to pieces invested with fine metalwork and stained glass.

Basic styles available from Ikea Tel. 44 181 208 5600
Larger, more elaborate pieces are available from the Conran Shop Tel. 44 171 589 7401

ANTIQUE

VASE

*It is difficult with Moroccan pottery to be precise about age and origin. Unlike silver, which is stamped by its maker, pottery was rarely marked. Thus, short of carbon-dating the glaze, age remains a mystery. In any case, it is extremely rare to come across one more than a hundred years old since Moroccan pottery was always made to be used. Ironically, this is a plus for collectors: quality and beauty alone determine value. If it's beautiful and not badly damaged … buy it. The **souks** of Marrakesh are the best place to buy old pottery, but you don't have to go yourself. 'Best of Morocco', an organization specializing in all aspects of travel to Morocco, can track down a piece (or pieces) for you.*

Best of Morocco Tel. 44 1380 828533

THÉ

À LA MENTHE

The serving of mint tea, a Moroccan speciality, is still very much a part of everyday life. Consumed throughout the day and especially after meals, mint tea is a great digestive. All that is required these days is the ubiquitous and quite distinctive teapot, small glasses, preferably hand-painted, some tea, sugar and fresh mint. On a hot day it is infinitely preferable to drinking coffee. It is also a custom that appears to be catching on abroad and you no longer have to go to Marrakesh to buy the distinctive Moroccan teapots or glasses.

Tables with tops of inlaid mosaic tiles are available from the Conran Shop Tel. 44 171 589 7401
Ikea and Designers Guild have a selection of teapots and hand-painted glasses (see above for telephone nos)

HOME

MOSAIC

*One of the most captivating and emotive aspects of Morocco is the vast and elaborate expanses of intricate and brightly coloured tiled mosaics that adorn the walls and floors of mosques, palaces and public spaces. The secret of their attraction lies in the extraordinary skills of the **zlayiyyah**, the **zillij** master who spends a lifetime devoted to this art form. Such spatial sophistication and decorative power are now available outside Morocco in the form of table tops, made in Morocco and then exported, and in architectural work from a few **zillij** craftsmen who now work for the Kasbah in London's Covent Garden.*

For table tops, the Conran Shop Tel. 44 171 589 7401
The Kasbah Tel. 44 171 240 3538

"Without doubt, Morocco, with one or two kingdoms in Asia,

represents the last surviving example of a civilization of the ancient world.

One finds here customs, moral and physical aspects of mankind

that are eternal, simply because they have never changed.

Constantly, watching a gesture of prayer or salutation,

a dance, a semi-naked beggar,

the way a tailor prepares his cloth,

a pilgrim following his donkey across the vast expanse of the bled,

or looking into the smoky shade of a mill

where occasional shafts of light pierce the tangle of beams,

we feel we have seen it all before…

For all the differences of appearance

they recall to us the essential identity of mankind.

If such a world, which shares so deeply the spirit of the past,

had disappeared two thousand years ago,

we would have lost a certain understanding of the past

and of ourselves, for we could never have recreated it…

But that it has survived until our times,

that we can see it, we can touch it, we can mix with its people,

is a miracle that never ceases to astonish."

André Chevrillon
Marrakesh dans les Palmes